BALANCING ACTS:

Community-Based Forest Management and National Law in Asia and the Pacific

Owen J. Lynch
Kirk Talbott

WORLD
RESOURCES
INSTITUTE

SEPTEMBER 1995

in collaboration with
Marshall S. Berdan, editor
Jonathan Lindsay and Chhatrapati Singh
   (India Case Study)
Chip Barber (Indonesia Case Study)
Shantam Khadka (Nepal Case Study)
Alan Marat (Papua New Guinea Case Study)
Janis Alcorn (Thailand Case Study)
Antoinette Royo-Fay (Philippines Case Study)
Lalanath de Silva and G.L. Anandalal
   Nanayakkara (Sri Lanka Case Study)

Library of Congress Cataloging-in-Publication Data

Lynch, Owen J. (Owen James)
 Balancing acts : community-based forest management and national law in Asia and the Pacific / Owen J. Lynch and Kirk Talbott with Marshall S. Berdan.
  p.   cm.
 Includes bibliographical references.
 ISBN 1-56973-033-4 (alk. paper)
 1. Forestry law and legislation—Asia. 2. Forestry law and legislation—Pacific Area. I. Talbott, Kirk, 1955– II. Berdan, Marshall S.   III. Title.
KNC768.L96   1995
346.504'675—dc20
[345.064675]   95-34925
                                                                      CIP

Kathleen Courrier
Publications Director

Brooks Belford
Marketing Manager

Hyacinth Billings
Production Manager

Lomangino Studio
Cover Design

Chip Fay
Cover Photos

Each World Resources Institute Report represents a timely, scholarly treatment of a subject of public concern. WRI takes responsibility for choosing the study topics and guaranteeing its authors and researchers freedom of inquiry. It also solicits and responds to the guidance of advisory panels and expert reviewers. Unless otherwise stated, however, all the interpretation and findings set forth in WRI publications are those of the authors.

Copyright © 1995 World Resources Institute. All rights reserved.
         Printed on recycled paper

... I have once taken as an example a law relating to land tenure and the livelihood of people in remote areas to whom we cannot apply the law because, through the authorities' fault due to their inability to reach them, the people have no means of knowing the law. The fault rests with the law-enforcing side rather than with the one upon which the law is to be enforced. This is quite a substantive point too. Ways must, therefore, be found to implement the law according to the dictates of nature. There is a particular legal matter which I have come across—a rather special one, but all the same, I should like to relate it, because it has given rise to complications. It also has to do with land tenure and people in remote areas. In forests designated and delineated by the authorities as reserved or restricted, there were people there already at the time of the delineation. It seems rather odd for us to enforce the reserved forest law on the people in the forest which became reserved only subsequently by the mere drawing of lines on pieces of paper. The problem arises inasmuch as, with the delineation done, these people became violators of the law. From the viewpoint of law, it is a violation, because the law was duly enacted; but according to natural law, the violator of the law is the one who drew the lines, because the people who had been in the forests previously possessed the human rights, meaning that the authorities had encroached upon individuals and not individuals transgressing the law of the land.

H.M. Bhumibol Adulyadej
King of Thailand

Excerpted from a royal statement delivered on June 27, 1973. Reprinted with royal permission.

CONTENTS

Foreword vii
Acknowledgments xi
Preface xiii

Introduction: Forests and People 1

I. **Deforestation and the Prospects for Community-Based Management** 9
    Forest Resource and Demographic Assessments 9
    Community-Based Management: Some Basic Considerations 23

II. **Historical Overview: Colonial Patterns of Forest Management** 31
    The Colonial Foundations 32
    Sri Lanka 34
    India 36
    Nepal 38
    Indonesia 40
    The Philippines 41
    Thailand 46
    The Rise of Asian Elites 48

III. **Contemporary Overview: The Legacies of State Ownership** 51
    The New Colonialists 51
    Indonesia 52
    Thailand 55

v

The Philippines 57
Sri Lanka.. 60
India 61
Nepal.. 64
In Sum... 65

IV. Community-Based Forest Management: Emerging Responses 67
India 69
Nepal.. 83
The Philippines 86
Thailand 92
Sri Lanka... 95
Indonesia 98
Lessons from Papua New Guinea 100

V. Recognizing Private Community-Based Rights......... 109
State Recognition Versus State Grants 116
Private Community-Based Rights 120

VI. Promoting Sustainable Forest Management Through Community-Based Tenure 125
Equitable Bargaining 125
Community Forest Leases 126
Information Dissemination 130
Informed Consent..................................... 130
Notice 131
Community and Legal Personalities 131
Third Parties... 132
Negotiations and Benefit Sharing...................... 133

Conclusion.. 135
About the Authors 137
Appendix A. Sample Forest Protection Lease............... 139
Appendix B. Sample Forest Community Lease 143
Notes 147
Bibliography 167

FOREWORD

An enduring source of food, shelter, fuel, and spiritual nourishment, tropical forests sustain hundreds of millions of people who live in or near them. In turn, many traditional forest-dwellers sustain the forests, drawing on local knowledge passed down over generations. Yet, most such people have little say in decisions about the fate of the forests. Laws all but silence them: most national governments in tropical Asia still abide by centralized forest-ownership systems inherited from the colonial past, systems in which the rights of forest-dwelling communities are not recognized.

To maintain healthy and productive forests, governments must build partnerships with the people who live in and from the forest and who have a direct stake in strategies to manage forest resources sustainably. Providing a rationale and a blueprint for such partnerships is *Balancing Acts: Community-Based Forest Management and National Law in Asia and the Pacific* by WRI Senior Associates Owen J. Lynch and Kirk Talbott, with assistance from Marshall S. Berdan and collaborating colleagues in the seven case-study countries. Capping five years of research on how national and state laws influence the fate of forests and forest-dwelling peoples, this report identifies laws and policies that could foster collaboration between governments and forest-dependent communities.

Balancing Acts surveys the historical antecedents and contemporary status of national laws and policies affecting forests and forest-dwellers in India, Indonesia, Nepal, the Philippines, Sri Lanka, Thailand, and Papua New Guinea. Besides numbering among Asia's and the Pacific's most heavily forested countries, all seven reflect the various legal, historical, and cultural settings under which community-based forest management initiatives are being forged—and, more important, being revised as environmental conditions deteriorate. Papua New Guinea is unique for its exemplary constitutional recognition of community-based management rights that promote wider distribution of forestry's benefits (though doesn't necessarily ensure sustainable or equitable forest-management practices). In all seven case studies, WRI's legal scholars collaborated with host-country counterparts.

The authors also discuss emerging programs in the case-study countries and review the theoretical framework of community-based property rights. They present model legal instruments and other recommendations for promoting sustainable community-based forest management. To show why nations should follow these guidelines, Lynch and Talbott argue that only by sharing power with local communities can overburdened national forest departments ensure the health and equitable development of the nation's forest patrimony.

Although no two nations face the same management constraints and opportunities, the comparative analysis offered in *Balancing Acts* yields lessons vital to any forested country. Indeed, the representatives from 14 Asian and Pacific nations who shared their experiences and insights at the project's 1994 workshop in the Philippines honed in on the same two principles that emerged from the case studies:

1. The national system of forest ownership and management that prevails throughout South and Southeast Asia is not sustaining forest stocks.
2. Securing local populations' community-based tenurial rights through a national policy and legal framework can improve forest management and enhance local incentives for sustainable development.

Across Asia, the authors recommend, the respective rights and duties of national governments and local communities should be balanced in mutually beneficial and enforceable ways. Now that many studies from Asia and the Pacific are documenting the causal link between secure tenure and forest health, the authors argue, the time is ripe for the changes they advocate.

Balancing Acts extends the analyses and recommendations set forth in such previous studies as *Breaking the Logjam: Obstacles to Forest Policy Reform in Indonesia and the United States*, *Surviving the Cut: Natural Forest Management in the Humid Tropics*, and *The Forest for the Trees: Government Policies and the Misuse of Forest Resources*. Building on this earlier work, *Balancing Acts* meets the pressing need for thorough country-by-country analyses of the political, social, and economic relationships between national governments and citizens who live in "public" forest zones.

We would like to thank the United States Agency for International Development, the Ford Foundation, and the International Development Research Centre for financial support of the research and fieldwork reflected in *Balancing Acts*. To all three, we are deeply grateful.

Jonathan Lash
President
World Resources Institute

ACKNOWLEDGMENTS

The authors thank the United States Agency for International Development's (USAID) Asia/Near East and Global Bureaus, and in particular Molly Kux and George Taylor, for encouragement, ideas, and financial support. Additional financial support for this work has been provided by the Ford Foundation and the International Development Research Centre, which also deserve thanks.

Special mention and appreciation is extended to the country case study co-authors: Jonathan Lindsay and Chhatrapati Singh (India); Chip Barber (Indonesia); Shantam Khadka (Nepal); Alan Marat (Papua New Guinea); Janis Alcorn (Thailand), Antoinette Royo-Fay (Philippines); and Lalanath de Silva and G.L. Anandalal Nanayakkara (Sri Lanka). Jon Lindsay was especially helpful in the drafting of *Balancing Acts*.

Among colleagues at World Resources Institute who provided valuable insights and other assistance are Jonathan Lash, Walt Reid, Tom Fox, Walter Arensberg, Robert Repetto, Janet Brown, Ann Thrupp, Mieke van der Wansem, Paul Faeth, Sarah Burns, Catherine Veninga, Audrey Im, and Nigel Sizer. Similar expertise was shared by the following external reviewers: Molly Kux, Daniel W. Bromley (who also contributed Box 4), Jeff Romm, Mark Poffenberger, Amrit L. Joshi, Augusta Molnar, and Mark Zimsky. Other important support was extended by H. Sheridan Plunkett, Chip Fay, Gregory Maggio, the Legal Rights and Natural Resources Center–Kasama sa Kalikasan (LRC-KSK) in the Philippines, and other who have chosen to remain anonymous.

Timely help creating an outreach plan for this book was volunteered by WRI's Policy Affairs group, especially William Visser and Michelle Corrigan.

Editorial assistance was generously and amiably provided first and foremost by Marshall S. Berdan, to whom the authors are forever indebted. Additional editorial and production help was consistently and graciously provided by Deborah Fort and Kathleen Courrier and her excellent team: Hyacinth Billings, Robbie Nichols, and Samantha Fields. The authors thank everyone for their contributions, but assume full responsibility for any errors or omissions.

O.J.L.
K.T.

PREFACE

In January 1990, the Center for International Development and Environment of the World Resources Institute inaugurated its Tenurial Policies and Natural Resources Management Project. The project's primary goal is to promote equity and help curb deforestation in developing countries by identifying national laws that establish or bolster viable short- and long-term community-based management incentives, particularly on so-called "public" or "state" lands. To accomplish this objective, the project has sought to identify and develop legal and policy strategies that will gain recognition for, and secure the tenurial rights and claims of, forest-dependent communities, preferably without resorting to the enactment of time-consuming, cumbersome, and politically contentious new legislation. Of particular concern are communities that manage their resources responsibly and sustainably.

The first phase of the project was to conduct national-level legal and policy analyses of community-based forest management in several South and Southeast Asian countries—India, Indonesia, Nepal, the Philippines, Sri Lanka, and Thailand—among the most important countries in Asia in terms of forest assets. They also reflect the various legal, historical, and cultural settings under which community-based forest management initiatives are being forged and, more important, revised as environmental conditions deteriorate. An additional study was undertaken in Papua New Guinea, where, in spite of constitutional recognition of community-based management rights, forests are also falling under the axes of unsustainable and inequitable practices.

Except for the case study conducted in Thailand, a Western legal scholar collaborated with host-country counterparts to identify the historical foundations for current national laws and to analyze how such laws are being used (or abused) in managing national forest resources. Although no two nations face the same resource management constraints and opportunities, the project's working assumption—that helpful and important lessons can result from comparative analysis—proved valid.

To build understanding of common problems and approaches, representatives from 14 Asian and Pacific nations convened at a workshop in Baguio City, the Philippines, in May 1994. With other advocates and practitioners of community-based forest management, they shared their experiences and insights and this report tries to reflect both.

The workshop participants identified three principles emerging from the case studies:

1. The prevailing paradigm of nation-state ownership and management of forest resources in South and Southeast Asia is not sustaining declining stocks of forest.
2. An alternative policy and legal framework that recognizes and secures local populations' private, community-based tenurial rights provides the best prospects for improving forest management.
3. Local authority and management structures need further development and refinement if the respective rights and correlative duties of nation-states and local communities are to be securely balanced.

Generally speaking, across Asia and much of the developing world, this balance tips, and state-sanctioned incentives for local sustainable management are inadequate. In many areas, only a legitimate, mutually enforceable, and secure balance between governments and local communities can arrest—and ultimately reverse current deforestation trends.

The practical connections between security of tenure and improved local forest-management practices clearly need additional research. But as long as nearly all officially sanctioned management systems in Asia are state centered, most traditional community-based systems will function without state sanction or any countervailing state authority.

Although perceived security of tenure is often enough to sustain community-based management systems, true tenurial security that includes state sanction is virtually unknown in the Asian region. As a result, no scientifically valid conclusions based upon comprehensive empirical studies of the connection between state sanction and local management incentives can yet be offered. Nevertheless, demonstrable connections between community-based tenurial rights and effective resource management are increasingly being recognized and studied. Anecdotal and historical evidence suggests that in many instances national resources are best managed locally. More important, numerous studies from Asia and the Pacific, as well as other regions, are beginning to document the causal linkages. One result is that local and national forestry projects are increasingly addressing tenurial issues.

To enhance understanding of how state-dominated forest-management systems actually work, this synthesis report surveys the historical antecedents and contemporary status of current national laws and policies. It includes a review of the theoretical framework of community-based property rights and a discussion of emerging programs in the case-study countries. The last two chapters contain substantive and procedural recommendations (including model legal instruments) for promoting sustainable community-based forest management.

Balancing Acts responds to the pressing need for improved country-by-country policy analyses of the political, social, and economic relationships between countries and local peoples living in "public" forest zones. Through this document, WRI's Center for International Development and Environment hopes to enhance national policy-makers' understanding of the problems and potential of forest-dependent communities. Its findings apply not only to the seven countries studied here, but to any country striving to promote sustainable development by balancing the rights and duties of national governments with those of forest-dependent communities.

Map of the Seven Case-Study Countries

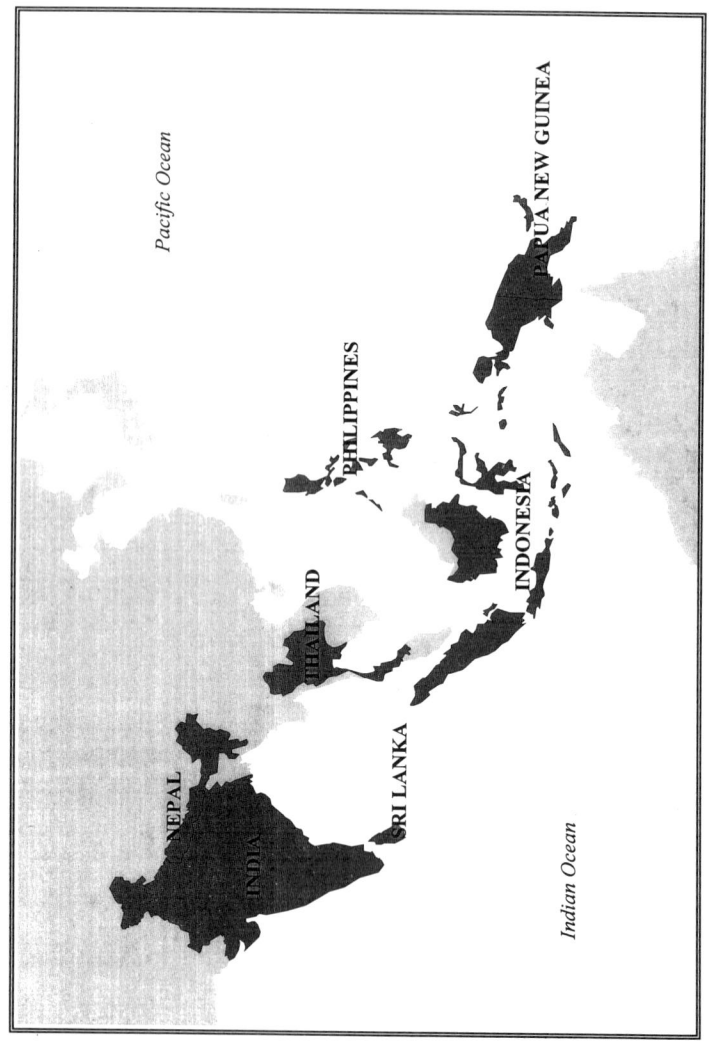

INTRODUCTION: FORESTS AND PEOPLE

The Asia and Pacific regions are large and diverse and include one-fourth of the world's tropical forests and approximately half of its biological species. Throughout South and Southeast Asia and the Pacific, however, vast tracts of forest lands have been degraded or denuded. In India, where population pressures and rapid industrialization have been particularly acute, forest cover has decreased since the 1850s from 40 percent to substantially less than 20 percent of total land area. At the turn of the century, Thailand, the Philippines, and Sri Lanka were about 70 percent covered with natural forests. Over the last century, that figure has shrunk to less than 25 percent.

Deforestation contributes to an array of environmental damages besides loss of biodiversity. These include soil erosion, siltation of riverine and coastal water systems, flooding, drought, harm to infrastructure, destruction of mangroves and both freshwater and saline fishing areas, and declines in agricultural productivity. Deforestation also reduces the carbon sink that forests provide, which helps mitigate global warming.

Well over a century ago, a number of concerned European colonists began to speak out against the deforestation caused by their own nations' colonial policies in South and Southeast Asia. In the mid-1860s, British forester Henry Cleghorn voiced alarm at the wanton deforestation born of colonial practices near Madras. The best way to preserve the subcontinent's remaining forests, he maintained, was to allow local villages to retain their traditional management systems. Who else, he argued, had as great an incentive or could maintain local forests more cheaply?[1] Fifty years later, the Dutch forester W. Groeneveldt called for a halt to the colonial administration's overzealous promotion of commercial coffee plantations on the Indonesian island of Java. His solution to the rampant degradation? A return to traditional community-based management.[2]

Given the industrial and technological advances of the past 150 years and steady population increases, the continuing depletion of the forests of South and Southeast Asia was perhaps inevitable. Since 1901, India's population has more than tripled and Indonesia's has grown by only slightly less.[3] Similar increases have occurred in other countries in the region. National resource bases have been overused as technological advances have brought progressively higher standards of living. Although there is no denying that meeting the needs of increasing populations has played a substantial role in reducing original forest cover, prevailing management practices have made those losses worse. Practices decried long ago by critics like Cleghorn and Groeneveldt have continued virtually unabated and have made it all but impossible to sustain increasingly scarce—and thus increasingly valuable—forest resources.

Uncontrolled—and all too often illegal—logging accounts for much of the deforestation. Testifying to the fact that the days of uncontrolled extraction are numbered, commercial logging in natural forests is now banned in Thailand, Cambodia, and parts of India, and it is severely restricted in the Philippines.

In Indonesia and the Pacific nation of Papua New Guinea, however, commercial logging continues largely unabated. The Indonesian situation is particularly alarming: in 1950, some 84 percent of the newly independent nation's extensive territory was blanketed with forests. As of 1989, the official figure had been reduced to 60 percent and deforestation was believed to be proceeding at a pace of 1.3 million hectares, or one percent, per year.[4]

But the impact of forest loss is not limited to declines in timber industries' output. Besides threatening global reserves of biodiversity and damaging the carbon sinks that absorb greenhouse gases, degrading forest ecosystems jeopardizes the well-being of tens of millions of forest-dependent peoples. Most immediately, loss of access to their main sources of food, fuel, shelter, and clothing jeopardizes their livelihood and survival.

Forest-based populations are also threatened by the devastating environmental repercussions that come with forest loss or degradation. Loss of tree cover can accelerate natural erosion, choking waterways, setting off rockslides and landslides, and triggering floods more numerous and destructive than historical norms. Although all these common conditions are debilitating and compromising, typically only disasters, such as flash floods, grab headlines and center world attention on the human costs of deforestation.

In November 1989, floods swept down denuded hillsides in southern Thailand, carrying more than 300 people to their deaths, and riveted national attention on excessive commercial logging. In response to widespread vocal criticism the Thai government banned commercial logging six weeks after the disaster.[5] Three years later on the Philippine island of Leyte, storm waters rushed down once-forested river valleys, killing 5,000.[6] The primary cause of this tragedy was the deforestation that had occurred over the past 30 years as extensive tracts of forest gave way to plantation agriculture. And, in the summer of 1993, prolonged monsoonal rains in Nepal and India resulted in floods that would eventually claim the lives of more than 2,000 people. Once again, deforestation was singled out as the precipitating factor, not of the rains that fell, but of the severity of the floods that ensued.[7]

What recurring scenarios such as these tell us is that some so-called "natural disasters" don't just happen. They are often the outcome of unsustainable patterns of resource usage and human interactions that have long been in the making.

Although historical records are scarce, indigenous Asian states and kingdoms existed long before the colonial conquests exploited—and in some localities, overexploited—their forests. Given the limited extent of these pre-colonial impositions in absolute terms, the vastness of the original forest domain, and the usually prodigious rates of natural regeneration, these claims on nature's patrimony could generally be accommodated without jeopardizing ecosystems. But however environmentally benign, early Asian societies—like their counterparts elsewhere—were not necessarily equitable or just, at least not by the standards of late 20th-century democracies.

Whether it was for the good of the greater society or the benefit of the ruling authority, most forest-dependent people have long been deprived of an equitable share of forest resources. Starting in the 15th century, European colonial powers with their advanced technology began repeating patterns of exploitation already common in South and Southeast Asia. New kinds of weapons allowed colonial powers to seize what they wanted; ships, wagons, and trains helped them to carry away their booty. Well armed and avaricious, the European colonists gradually changed from traders into masters, increasing their control over land resources and extracting more and more from their new colonies.

The colonial acquisition of forest products and other natural resources was often accompanied by the legal expropriation—at least in the minds of the colonizers—of the sovereignty and property rights of indigenous populations. Prevailing conceptions of Western (Roman) law, which had come to dominate contemporary European jurisprudence, were used by the colonizers to justify their use and abuse of natural resources, including forests.

Although similar legal expropriations took place at the hands of indigenous rulers (witness the history of Thailand, the one nation studied here that was never a European colony), pre-colonial exploitation was often tempered by traditional local resource management systems that were predicated on the belief that forests and other natural resources should serve the collective good. That good was promoted by adherence to usage rights and regulations promulgated and enforced by traditional leaders. The long-term survival of the entire community depended upon how prudently the surrounding resource base was used.

In sharp contrast, many colonial officials believed that they were entitled to expropriate and use natural resources by virtue of their innate cultural superiority. In fact, it was military superiority that gave the colonizers their greatest advantage. After World War II, the legal successors to the former colonial states—the political and economic elites of modern independent Asian nation-states—continued to rely on the colonial legal usurpations. Since then, forest laws and policies have generally been predicated on the assumption that the national interest is best served by trading natural resources for consumer goods in international marketplaces.

The legal usurpation of community-based tenurial rights has not necessarily ended communities' tenure. Despite expansive claims of ownership, national governments in South and Southeast Asia exercise relatively little control over many forest areas. Few can pay, train, or maintain the forest-department staff needed to survey, patrol, and manage the vast areas classified as public forest land effectively. In Indonesia, for example, a single forest officer is often responsible for 20,000 hectares and is largely without transportation and other basic professional tools.[8]

As exclusive state-management paradigms fail, in many locales once-vast forest resources have dwindled so much that they can no longer satisfy profit-oriented extractive and commercial industries, be they state or privately run. As forest resources disappear, so do once-thriving timber industries. The depletion of national reserves also means that many rural Asians are increasingly hard-pressed to meet their daily needs. Especially vulnerable are historically marginalized, indigenous, and tribal peoples who still live outside mainstream society. For centuries, when their traditional areas were infringed by more powerful local cultures, they retreated farther and farther into the forests. But today, there are few places left to hide.

Unable to secure an equitable balance of rights and duties in the nation-states in which they dwell, many forest-dependent peoples have no choice but to assert control over their forests—either quietly or defiantly. In light of numerous and increasingly well publicized instances of deforestation and its effects, even the most entrenched of centralized Asian governments have begun to acknowledge the failure of state-managed systems and the need for greater community involvement. Throughout the region, new policies and programs with names such as "social forestry," "community forestry," and "joint forest management" are emerging.

In northern India in the early 1970s, important social movements among forest-dependent peoples showed the world both the adverse social and environmental devastation being wrought by government forest policies and the potential benefits of community management. The most celebrated was the Chipko movement in northern India where women put their arms around trees targeted for cutting by commercial loggers. More than a protest, the Chipko movement was an assertion of community control over forest resources.

These movements helped prompt West Bengal and other state forest departments to explore the potential of sharing the management of government forests with local communities. Today, over 350,000 hectares of degraded forests in India are being co-managed, and the results have largely been positive.

Similar experiments and programs have followed in other South and Southeast Asian countries as national governments belatedly began to realize that established precepts of state management and control were in many cases actually contributing to the demise of remaining forest resources.

The net result of all these initiatives is emerging support for local forest management. The pendulum of policy in many countries—both within and outside of Asia—is swinging back toward recognizing traditional community-based rights. Although such readjustments have often sprung more from environmental concerns than from deep-seated commitments to equity, they are still a welcome and encouraging change. The current challenge is to continue the process and discover the balance that holds the best promise for sustainable management of diminishing forest resources.

The simple fact is that involving local populations, especially long-term residents, in forest management makes good sense. It provides those most knowledgeable about the local resource base with official incentives for sustainable use. It likwise empowers them to police the forest and prevent outsiders and members of their own communities from overexploiting forest resources. In other words, "the logic of community forestry goes far beyond the patronizing view that community forestry means letting the local people get some benefits from the forest." Rather, it provides a means to "create and maintain a system of forest practices that are both ecologically and economically sustainable."[9]

Despite the enduring legal disenfranchisement of forest-dependent people, many Asian countries already have legal frameworks that support community-based forest management. Whether through newly devised regulations and procedures (as in Nepal and India), or through the rediscovery of long-ignored laws and constitutional provisions (as in the Philippines and, to a lesser extent, Indonesia), community-based forest management is gaining force and legitimacy throughout South and Southeast Asia. Unfortunately, in much of Asia, such laws are routinely ignored or circumvented, so forest dwellers and forest-dependent communities continue to be marginalized by national governments. This happens in three ways:

- official census reports underestimate the population of classified forest areas;
- forest-dependent peoples, including indigenous groups, are treated as illegal users of public resources; and
- forest-dependent peoples are stereotyped as environmentally destructive, slash-and-burn farmers.[10]

Where procedures do allow forest communities to attain official recognition and document their community-based property rights, the processes tend to be complex, time-consuming, and costly—virtually prohibitive barriers, especially for remote subsistence-oriented forest communities. Such obstacles allow politically well-connected outsiders to take advantage of administrative power structures in national or regional capitals to acquire documented rights over occupied forestlands.

Despite the increasing attention being given to community-based forest management in theory, real on-the-ground progress still lags. Data and analysis from the six Asian countries studied here indicate that current government incentives for sustainable community-based management of forest resources lack the scope and momentum needed to succeed. Because many communities don't have the legal and political leverage required to negotiate innovative and sustainable management strategies with economic and political elites, local groups essentially must take what they are offered. As a result, many programs that now fall under the rubric of community/social forestry are little more than short-term, renewable (and cancelable) contract-based reforestation initiatives.

As national forest resources dwindle and community-based management programs are finally being considered with some urgency, national governments should establish effective and enforceable administrative processes that will facilitate the creation of authentic partnerships. The key word is "partnerships." This report neither suggests nor implies that national and state authorities have no role in managing forest resources. Cutting local communities in does not mean cutting governments and private businesses out. Rather, national, state, and local governments, as well as private companies and forest-dependent communities all have a vital role to play. A continuation of past policies, meanwhile, will only further the loss of increasingly scarce forest resources.

Anecdotal and, for now, inconclusive evidence from the field suggests that a better alternative would be to take advantage of the experiences and insights of the millions of forest-dependent people who have been using the forests for generations, but who find their existence increasingly jeopardized by short-sighted and unsustainable forestry practices.

I.
DEFORESTATION AND THE PROSPECTS FOR COMMUNITY-BASED MANAGEMENT

Forest Resource and Demographic Assessments

The current condition of forests in southern Asia and the Pacific cannot yet be assessed accurately. Some countries have required forest inventories, but none have dedicated the energy and financial resources needed to carry them out. Indonesia, for example, hasn't carried out an official forest inventory since 1950.[11] No doubt some governments don't want to quantify their inability to protect and rehabilitate forest resources: by not documenting current conditions, they minimize the ire of domestic public opinion and international monitors concerned about deforestation. Strained finances and understaffing in most national forest departments are also partly to blame.

But perhaps the main reason that data is not gathered is that nation-states want to retain legal jurisdiction over classified public forest land. With large portions of national territory entrusted to state care simply because the land is legally classified as forest, accurate assessments would weaken forest departments' jurisdiction and reduce already meager budgetary allotments. And so, to maintain their wide-ranging authority, forest departments and their patrons and beneficiaries perpetuate the fiction that many denuded or converted areas are still part of the national forest domain.

Forest departments, and hence national and state governments, tend to overestimate the extent and quality of national forest cover by using samplings from which extrapolations are impossible and relying on optimistic or outdated information. In the absence of alternative figures, these fictional statistics tend to be recycled and repackaged in international forums as fact. That said,

Box 1. Basic Forest Statistics: The Case of Thailand

The difficulties in determining the extent of Thailand's forests illustrate some of the pitfalls inherent in quantifying and qualifying national forest resources. Estimates of the current extent of tree cover in Thailand and most other countries—the basic statistic on the status and health of a country's forest resources—vary dramatically. The Royal Forest Department's 1991 assessment concluded that 26.6 percent of the country is covered by forests, while the Department of Land Development reported the same year that a more accurate figure was 34.4 percent.[a] Environmental groups, meanwhile, claimed that only about a sixth of the country was still forested.[b]

Both technical and political factors shed light on this discrepancy. The former stem from differing definitions of what constitutes forests and forest cover, as well as difficulty in monitoring vegetative cover over the nation's 51.3 million hectares. Forests can be officially labeled "degraded" on little, if any, empirical basis. Thailand's forests are sometimes classified as "degraded" because they do not contain enough high-grade timber to be profitable to logging operations. Biologists, in contrast, define them as diverse secondary forests recovering from logging and agricultural activities. Similarly, local farmers view the same woodlands as resource-rich parts of the agricultural systems that support them.[c] But biologists and local people rarely have a say in how land is classified.

The political factors behind the classification of a particular tract of government-owned forest land as "degraded" are also important. The Royal Forest Department profits from the degraded classification—interpreted as impossible to reforest—since it can lease such land to commercial entrepreneurs and agroforestry concerns. Often, when it does, occupants are displaced and natural secondary forests are quickly converted into plantations—a trend likely to be reinforced by a 1992 law promoting forest plantations that extends coverage to degraded forests.[d]

Given the potential importance of law on forest plantations, empirically based definitions of "degraded" and "forest" are essential if the terms are to be applied with any consistency. "Degraded" should not simply mean logged or cleared. Nor should "forest" describe

Box 1. (continued)

areas where a certain number of standing trees grow. Woodlands that are renewing—or are untouched—are "forests." And forests are "degraded" only if they are not undergoing healthy and sustainable regeneration.

Notes
a. Thai Forestry Sector Master Plan, vol. 5, p. 24 (1993). Royal Forest Department, *Forest Cover in Thailand in 1988*, 3. This official estimate is based on aerial photographs and LANDSAT imagery. Persistent cloud cover in some areas makes it necessary to rely on estimates for computing the national percentage.
b. Unofficial estimates are based on Norani Visetbhakdi, "Deforestation and Reforestation in Thailand," *Bangkok Bank Monthly Review* 243 (June 1989), and Pisit na Patalung, personal communication, 1992.
c. Willemine Brinkman, ed. *Why Natural Forests are Linked with Nutrition, Health, and Self-Reliance of Villagers in Northeast Thailand: Phu Wiang, Khon Kaen Province* Fo: DP/THA/84/00W Field Document 6 (Bangkok: Royal Forest Department, United Nations Development Programme, and Food and Agriculture Organization of the United Nations, 1989); Lert Chuntanaparb and Henry I. Wood, *Management of Degraded Forest Land in Thailand* (Bangkok: Kasetsart University, 1986); P. Sanguantam, Lert Chuntanaparb, and P. Prasomsin, *Multi-Resource Inventories in Dong Mun Forest Communities, Northeast Thailand* 870-0535 Working Document No. 3 (Bangkok: Kesetsart University/Ford Foundation , 1988); Sanitsuda Ekachai, *Behind the Smile: Voices of Thailand* (Bangkok: Post Publishing, 1990), 41.
d. One can ensure that a patch of forest land is classified as degraded in various ways. A common method is to include forested and deforested areas in one classification tract—basically calculating an average trees-per-hectare figure that can be applied to a large tract encompassing areas still forested. Another way is to actually degrade the area by cutting down a certain number of trees. Larry Lohmann, private communication, 1991.

even official rose-colored statistics from South and Southeast Asia paint a dismal picture. *(See Table 1.)* According to the *World Resources Report 1995*, annual deforestation in insular Southeast Asia averaged 1.2 percent between 1981 and 1990—almost twice the global average of 0.8 percent. This corresponds to a total loss of 3.9 million hectares in one decade. In Thailand and the Philippines, the annual rate was 2.9 percent, over three-and-a-half times the global average. Although percentages are falling in absolute terms, nearly four times as much forest was actually lost in Indonesia, one of the largest remaining national repositories of forest resources in the world, than in Thailand and the Philippines.

For South Asia, the figures are somewhat better: annual deforestation for the same decade was estimated at 0.8 percent—the global average. Keep in mind, though, that most of the primary and secondary forests of India, Pakistan, Sri Lanka, and Bangladesh were cleared well before the 1980s. The bottom line? Forest resources in South and Southeast Asia are fast disappearing.

Table 1. Forest Resources

GOVERNMENT STATISTICS

Nation	1990 Extent ('000 hectares)	Forest Cover % of National Territory	% Annual Deforestation 1981–90 ('000 hectares)	Annual Loss ('000 hectares)
India	51,729	17.4	.06	339
Indonesia	109,549	60.5	1.0	1,212
Nepal	5,023	36.7	1.0	55
Philippines	7,831	26.3	2.9	316
Sri Lanka	1,746	27.0	1.3	27
Thailand	12,735	24.9	2.9	515

Source: World Resources Report 1994–1995, pp. 306–307.

On-the-ground estimates made by environmental organizations may offer the most accurate picture of the region's forest resources, even though these groups are often constrained by limited access to official sources, and work with limited financial resources. According to some Thai environmental groups, for example, forest cover in Thailand ranges between 10 and 17 percent, at least 10 percent below the government's figure of 28 percent.[12]

As of 1994, the Forest Management Bureau in the Philippines still contends that over 15 million hectares—more than half the nation's land mass—is either classified as "public" forest or legally presumed to be. According to a 1989 World Bank estimate, however, only six million hectares contained "any significant tree cover" and only one million hectares were "productive, old growth forest."[13] Clearly, the situation is far worse than official statistics suggest.

Through technological advances in satellite imagery, it may be possible to know, within a small margin of statistical error, the nature and extent of forest cover in Asia and across the globe. Meanwhile, it is apparent that forest resources in South and Southeast Asia are continuing their century-long decline. Burgeoning national populations and their growing demands on forest resources to meet the need for food, energy, and shelter, intensify the pressures.

Although the dynamics of deforestation in each of the seven countries studied are determined by each nation's unique history and forest resources, regional similarities abound. All share geological and climatic conditions, and all (except for Thailand) were ruled by Western colonial powers. And all rely increasingly on international market forces.

During Asia's colonial era, benefits from extensive natural forests—which were reduced by commercial extraction and agricultural conversion—went largely to commercial cartels and metropolitan coffers. World War II laid waste portions of South and Southeast Asia's forests: fierce and destructive fighting and forced contributions to war efforts depleted forest resources. Then, beginning in the late 1940s, forest resources fed the industrialization and modernization of independent nation-states.

One legacy of the colonial period was the emergence of national economies based largely on the extraction of natural resources. Combined with the devastation of national infrastructures and heightened postwar demands for raw materials, extractive economics became even more virulent after independence. High demand for timber and wood products from the new economic dynamos of East Asia—particularly Japan, Taiwan, and South Korea—reinforced this pattern. With highly protected or limited forest resources of their own, these three nations have continued to seek timber resources abroad. In Southeast Asia and, more recently, in the Pacific Island nations, governments eager to generate foreign exchange earnings have made ready partners. Indeed, Asian governments have been all too willing to sell off forest assets at prices well below market value,[14] while largely ignoring the hardships that commercial forest concessions impose on the lives and well-being of hundreds of thousands of forest-dependent citizens.

Countries with the most developed infrastructures and the strongest commercial ties to Western nations were the first to see their trees fall to the logging axes. Throughout the 1960s and 1970s the Philippines was the number-one timber supplier to the Japanese, with Thailand also providing a steady source of supply. In the 1980s as these resources diminished, primary supply lines shifted to Indonesia and Malaysia. The newest major timber pipeline is Papua New Guinea.

Of course, there is more to current deforestation trends in Southeast Asia than commercial logging. Although their relative impacts are difficult, if not impossible, to assess, small-scale and illegal logging and agricultural conversion play dominant and intertwining roles. With the development of roads, port facilities, and other infrastructure, and technological advances, including chain saws and bulldozers, large-scale logging and farming industries are rapidly penetrating Southeast Asia's remaining forests. Logging roads open up inaccessible areas to impoverished and landless farmers, fuelwood collectors, and extractors of non-timber forest products.[15]

Poverty also plays a role in deforestation, but the extent of its impact is often determined by factors other than sheer numbers of people. *(See Box 2.)* Governments obfuscating their own extractive practices, however, continue to single out swidden agriculture as the primary cause of national deforestation.

Governments in South and Southeast Asia and elsewhere have cast nearly all blame for their deforestation crises on forest

Box 2. Population and Deforestation—A Clear-Cut Connection?

Studies of the dynamics of contemporary forest-management practices reveal that deforestation stems from a variety of reasons. The relative weight of these factors varies not only from country to country, but also from area to area. Although most analyses identify population growth as one determinant of deforestation, considerable disagreement exists on the magnitude and direction of the causal link. The vast diversity of ecological conditions in the countries studied here help illustrate the polemics of this debate.

The connection between deforestation and population dynamics is rarely as clear cut as in Nepal, a mountainous country with limited arable land resources and a steady annual population growth rate of 2.5 percent. Ninety percent of the population is rural and survives on subsistence agriculture.[a] The size of the average family farm has dropped to less than one hectare—too small to support the average family of six under present agricultural conditions. Threatened by hunger, the typical farmer has little recourse but to convert sloping forest lands into additional fields—even though doing so decreases the availability of fuelwood, fodder, and other forest products.[b]

The Philippines is another country where large timber concessions exert more pressure on forests than local requirements for subsistence do. As one scholar concluded, "deforestation in the postwar Philippines is the result of two major processes: the conversion of primary to secondary forests through logging, and the removal of secondary forests by the expansion of agriculture" (1992). Behind these two factors is the "virtually unrestricted access" to forests by timber concessions issued to powerful Filipinos by the national government.[c]

Jack Westoby, former head of forestry at the United Nation's Food and Agriculture Organization, noted the complexity of interaction between population and forest as follows:

> There is no simple relationship between the extent of the forests and the size and distribution of the human population. Instances can be found in which large numbers of people live in harmony with their forests, and others where forests are devastated although few people are present.... It is not so much the number of human beings that has the crucial impact as the way in which human society is organized.[d]

> **Box 2.** (continued)
>
> Estimates vary widely, but it is safe to say that hundreds of millions of forest dwellers in Asia rely upon swidden cultivation.[e] Yale anthropologist Harold Conklin, whose seminal book on swidden agriculture in 1957 contains a formula for computing the human carrying capacity of swidden agriculture in tropical forests,[f] concluded that "in any given region, there can be no absolute carrying capacity, but only one which is relative to a particular system of land utilization."[g] More recently, Terry Rambo of the East-West Center, has argued that shifting cultivation is sustainable in the average tropical forest only as long as population densities remain below .4 person per hectare.[h]
>
> Compounding the complex interaction between population and deforestation are indirect correlations. Growing demands from urban, suburban, and rural people encourage those living near the forest to produce additional quantities of agricultural and wood products. In addition, the higher the standard of living of those wanting more goods, the greater the pressures on natural resources. These pressures can emerge not only from within the forested country but also from outside. Even modest population growth in the most developed countries, for example, can mean substantially higher demands for furniture, produce, gems, and other consumer goods based on tropical forest resources. Growth in faraway lands can have direct impacts as well. For example, when golf became both popular and prohibitively expensive in Japan and Taiwan, resort facilities were carved out of the forests of Thailand, Indonesia, and the Philippines.[i]
>
> **Notes**
> a. Paul R. Ehrlich, Anne H. Ehrlich, and Gretchen C. Daily, "Food Security, Population, and Environment," *Population and Development Review*, March 1993, vol. 19, no. 1:12.

dwellers who cultivate marginal lands.[16] In the Philippines, the government cites recent high rates of internal upland migration, due largely to poverty and land deprivation, as the primary factor.[17] In its 1991 report to the United Nations Conference on Environment and Development, the government of Sri Lanka noted

> **Box 2.** (continued)
>
> b. Jefferson Fox, "Forest Resources in a Nepali Village in 1980 and 1990: The Positive Influence of Population Growth," *Mountain Research and Development* (1993), vol. 13, no. 1:89–98.
> c. David M. Kummer, *Deforestation in the Postwar Philippines* (Quezon City, Philippines: Ateneo de Manila University Press, 1992): 99. *See also* David M. Kummer, "The Political Use of Philippine Forestry Statistics in the Postwar Period," *Crime, Law & Social Change* (1995), vol. 22, no. 163:180.
> d. Jack Westoby, *Introduction to World Forestry* (Oxford: Basil Blackwell, 1988):vii–viii and 137.
> e. Jean-Paul Lanley, *Tropical Forest Resources*, FAO Forestry Paper No. 30 (Rome: Food and Agriculture Organization of the United Nations, 1992), and Owen J. Lynch and Janis B. Alcorn, "Tenurial Rights and Community-Based Conservation," in David Western and R. Michael Wright, eds., *Natural Connections: Perspectives in Community-Based Conservation* (Washington, D.C. and Covelo, CA: Island Press, 1994):373–392.
> f. Critical population size = maximum cultivatable land ÷ minimum average area required for clearing/year.individual × minimum average duration of a full agricultural cycle.
> g. Harold C. Conklin, "Population-Land Balance Under Systems of Tropical Forest Agriculture," in *Proceedings of the Ninth Pacific Science Congress*, 1957 7 (1959):63.
> h. Terry Rambo, "Slash and Burn Farmers: Villains or Victims?," *Earthwatch*, No. 39 (3rd Quarter 1990):10–12.
> i. In what is perhaps an ultimate irony, the lands that once belonged to Mateo Cariño, the original plaintiff of ancestral domain claims in the Philippines *(see Box 5)*, are now in danger of being converted to a golf resort owned and operated by a Taiwanese conglomerate for the benefit of Taiwanese tourists.

that swidden cultivation (known locally as chena) produces nearly 80 percent of the country's rainfed grains and vegetables and provides livelihood for about 250,000 families, but has "disastrous" efffects and accounts for "the decline in the area and the quality of the forests."[18] *(See Box 3)*.

Box 3. Swidden Agriculture

Swidden agriculture—also known as slash-and-burn agriculture, shifting cultivation, jhum (India), *bhasme* (Nepal), *kaingin* (the Philippines), *chena* (Sri Lanka)—has sustained rural people around the globe for millenia. A growing number of studies show that swidden agriculture is not only ecologically sustainable in many circumstances, but is also often the most appropriate form of agriculture in forest areas, given the generally shallow and nutrient-poor nature of most upland tropical soils.[a]

Since the colonial era, swidden agriculture has been indiscriminately blamed as a—if not the—primary cause of deforestation. Much of this prejudice reflects ignorance: European colonists, familiar only with the sedentary agriculture practiced in most temperate climates, were dismayed to see tracts of dense forest land burned, converted, and then abandoned with apparent disregard. Adding to distaste for the practice, it was difficult, if not impossible, to tax. The Dutch characterized swidden agriculture as a "robber economy" and attempted to penalize it out of existence in Java and Sri Lanka. In the Philippines, it was denounced first by the Spanish and later by Americans, who enacted prohibitive but essentially unenforceable laws against it. To this day, it is legally punishable in the Philippines by up to four years' imprisonment and fines of up to US$1,000.

Like any other management practice, swidden agriculture is not always sustainable. The essential distinction is between swiddeners who farm sustainably and those who do not—a difference expressed by the terms "integral" and "nonintegral."[b] Integral swiddeners tend to cut and burn secondary forest cover and use the ash to fertilize the cleared field. After two or three harvests of a variety of crops, the integral swiddener leaves the field fallow, thus allowing the forest and topsoil to regenerate before renewing the annual planting cycle.

Most nonintegral swiddeners or "shifting cultivators," by contrast, are migrant farmers who lack knowledge of local weather and soils. Few know about the ecological fragility of tropical forests with their limited nutrient-holding capacity and delicate topsoil. Consequently, few let the land rest long enough for it to renew itself, or recognize the rights of those whose land is currently in fallow. Instead, most try to establish fixed temporary farm sites that they must

Box 3. (continued)

abandon after parching and erosion renders the land unproductive—in some cases, permanently.

Besides frequently using sophisticated agricultural techniques, communities operating integral swidden systems often manage a wide range of nonagricultural resources in ecologically sound ways. For example, they may practice agroforestry, maintain freshwater fisheries, manage harvests of non-timber forest products and game, and protect sacred forests. Studies demonstrate that, at least in some instances, integral swiddeners contribute more in the long run to a nation's gross national product than do capital-intensive extraction enterprises.[c]

Unfortunately, integral swidden agricultural systems are increasingly threatened by many of the same forces that cause deforestation. Naturally increasing populations, swelling numbers of migrants, and governmental propensities to issue forest concessions over large tracts of inhabited land disrupt the practices of many integral swiddeners. As a result, large numbers are being forced to shorten their fallow periods or to adapt to expensive agricultural technology and markets. All too often, the environment then erodes along with the knowledge bases that have long enabled local populations to practice sustainable agriculture.

Compounding these demographic and economic problems, most governments and forest policies fail to distinguish between integral and nonintegral swiddeners. Both are lumped together and indiscriminately blamed for the major share of national deforestation. Unfortunately, subsistence farmers (whether swiddeners or not) number among the most politically marginalized of citizens, while those responsible for the large-scale extraction of timber and cash crops tend to be among the most powerful—politically, economically, and socially. One of the easiest rationalizations for exporting natural resources comes from the lingering but mistaken colonial-era belief that swidden agriculture is invariably pernicious and irresponsible.

Notes
a. For a global overview and analysis *see* Lori Ann Thrupp, Susanna Hecht, Owen Lynch, and John Browder, *The Diversity and Dynamics of Shifting Cultivation: Myths, Realities, and the Political Ecology of*

> **Box 3.** (continued)
>
> *Changing Land Use in the Tropics* (Washinghton, D.C.: World Resources Institute, forthcoming 1996).
> b. This insight was first published in Harold C. Conklin's *Hanunoo Agriculture: A Report on an Integral System of Swidden Cultivation in the Philippines.* (Rome: Food and Agriculture Organization of the United Nations, 1957.) For more recent insights see sources cited in endnote 27.

Unauthorized agricultural conversion abetted by annual population increases in the range of 2 percent is responsible for some deforestation. But poor upland farmers in Asia and the Pacific are hardly the primary agents. Industrial and manufacturing centers absorb some of the landless rural poor, but increasingly dismal living conditions have weakened the lure of urban areas. Meanwhile, the concentration of legal rights to arable land resources in the hands of relatively few people has left little for acquisition—legally or otherwise—by cash-poor, landless farmers. Many believe that they have no alternative but to migrate into forest areas.[19]

At the same time, the nation-states of South and Southeast Asia have mimicked their colonial predecessors and asserted legal control over substantial portions of their territories by declaring vast areas—many of them inhabited—to be publicly owned forests *(See Table 2)*. Indonesia claims as much as 70 percent of the nation's land mass, for example, while the Philippine government considers itself the owner of more than half of the archipelago's land area. Indeed, private ownership of forest land, whether individual or community-based, is minimal throughout the region.

Just as governments maintain fictions about the extent of forests, they also deny or underestimate how their decisions affect the millions of people living in these so-called forest areas. Government officials are reluctant to acknowledge that, contrary to national law, many citizens occupy forest reserves. By ignoring or undercounting this number, governments can shirk responsibility for the well-being of these citizens and more easily grant rights to forest resources to commercial entrepreneurs.

Table 2. State Authority Over Forest Lands

	State-Owned Forest Land as a Percent of the National Territory	Percent of the National Territory Actually Forested	Percent of the National Territory Privately Owned
India	23	17.4	3
Indonesia	70	60.5	0
Nepal		36.7	<5
Philippines	53	26.3	2
Sri Lanka	68	27.0	<5
Thailand	40	24.9	

Note: Figures are based on official government statistics.

In all six of the Asian countries studied here, the government fails to compile complete, accurate, up-to-date, country-specific demographic studies of rural people living in or directly dependent on forests.[20] Rough but reasonable estimates made by non-governmental sources place in the hundreds of millions the number of people in these countries who either depend directly on forest resources or live on often degraded land classified as public forest. *(See Table 3)*. These estimates include a dwindling number (probably in the hundreds of thousands) of hunter-gatherers and pastoralists (most of whom live in India, where they make up 6 percent of the national population, or approximately 45 to 50 million people).

The exact number of forest-dependent people in South and Southeast Asia is impossible to determine. Whatever their numbers, most of their governments consider them to be squatters, illegally using state-owned resources, no matter how long they have occupied the forest. As such, they can be arbitrarily displaced, often with state sanction. The threat ripens into eviction when government officials grant outsiders commercial concessions to extract or

Table 3. Non-Governmental Estimates of Forest-Dependent Populations

Nation	Peoples Directly Dependent upon Forest Resources (millions)	Peoples Living on Land Classified as Public Forest (millions)
India	275	100
Indonesia	80–95	40–65
Nepal	18	8.5
Philippines	25–30	24
Sri Lanka	2-4	??
Thailand	20-25	14–16

Source: Owen J. Lynch, "Securing Community-Based Tenurial Rights in the Tropical Forests of Asia: An Overview of Current and Prospective Strategies," World Resources Institute, Washington, D.C., 1992, and subsequent updates by case study authors.

control natural resources in areas forest dwellers already occupy and use.

In some cases, displacement comes at the hands of government-mandated resettlement schemes. By far the most conspicuous of these has been Indonesia's Transmigration Program.[a] In the past 25 years, roughly two million Javanese and Balinese have relocated under this program to the outer islands of Sumatra, Sulawese, Kalimantan, and Irian Jaya.[21]

Underlying the legal claims of any nation-state to ownership of classified forest areas is the tacit assumption that those who have been using the resource base, in many cases for hundreds of years, are not necessarily those who should be entrusted with its continued management. Looking for quick economic returns, national

---

[a.] In response to widespread public criticism, the World Bank no longer provides financial support for Indonesian Transmigration.

governments in Southeast Asia undervalue the often sustainable practices of millions of forest-dependent peoples, primarily because such practices do not generate much hard revenue or tax money.

Studies have demonstrated that, over time, subsistence-level economies can in some instances contribute more to a nation's gross domestic product and to social equity than capital-intensive extraction enterprises.[22] But rather than taking the long view, national governments continue to issue concessions and licenses to capital-intensive enterprises, especially timber-extraction operations and agricultural plantations. The inability of Asian governments to appreciate gray market revenues, to wait for delayed economic returns, or to value conservation in its own right undermines local-level management capacities. This myopia also promotes the overexploitation of marketable natural resources. Indeed, many right-holders maximize short-term returns from land they rarely, if ever, visit.

Community-Based Management: Some Basic Considerations

Debate in Asia and the Pacific over the scope and definition of "community forestry" is ongoing and intensifying.[b] Should the concept be applied to forestry not initiated by villagers to meet their own needs and opportunities? Should it cover programs designed by outsiders to fit what they think are villagers' needs or to meet targets set by external organizations? Or should community-based forestry management refer—as it does in this book—only to internally initiated and maintained endeavors?

More and more evidence (which goes well beyond anecdotal) shows that for generations forest-dependent people have sustainably managed forest resources through community-based systems.[23]

---

[b] This book employs the definition of community that is adopted by Herman Daly and John Cobb in *For the Common Good* at pp. 168–175. It calls for: 1) extensive participation by its members in the decisions by which its life is governed; 2) the community as a whole takes responsibilities for its members; and 3) this responsibility includes respect for the diverse individuality of these members.

That so many of these systems continue to function, albeit often in altered forms, testifies to their efficacy and resiliency. That they are actually undergoing a resurgence, especially in South Asia, signifies the failure of state-managed systems to address the basic needs of forest-dependent people.

Contrary to enduring stereotypes, sustainable community-based management systems are operated neither by ecological "noble savages" living in symbiotic harmony with nature, nor by self-centered exploiters seeking to maximize short-term gain. Like participants in other sustainable systems, most successful community-based managers are rational strategic-minded individuals who assess existing conditions and act in their own best interests. The more they depend upon the surrounding resource base, the more incentive they have to protect it. If their very survival is predicated upon maintaining it, they will do so unless prevented by ineluctable forces. In that case, they either fight or move on.[24]

The characteristics of community-based tenurial rights vary. They are often distinguishable from Western property concepts, which are based largely on state-created, private, individual rights. Community-based tenurial rights are not the equivalent of "open access" regimes.[25] They include individual and group rights, and typically derive from long-term relationships established between local peoples and the natural resources that sustain them.

Unlike their state-sanctioned individual counterparts, community-based rights often derive from the precept that the present generation holds the natural resource base, including forests, in trust for future generations. The privileges of the individual are thus generally subservient to the rights of the greater community (a situation that likewise prevails among most governments and their citizens). In addition, an individual's freedom is predicated upon the productive use of natural resources. By ensuring that they are carefully managed and the rights to them are equitably allocated, community-based tenurial rights contribute both to cultural and national continuity.

Functionally, community-based management systems and the property rights that they establish and support draw their fundamental legitimacy from the community in which they operate rather than from the nation-state in which they are located. Regardless of whether the system covers private or public land, community members—not government officials or employees of nongovernmental organizations or development institutions—are the primary (but not necessarily the sole) allocators and enforcers of community-based rights. Here, community-based management is thus invoked only in reference to initiatives that are primarily controlled and legitimated from within a community. Externally initiated activities with varying degrees of community participation should not be referred to as community-based, at least not until the community exercises primary decision-making authority.[26]

Much outside support for community-based management systems reflects the assumption that those who have lived in an area for a long time have the best working knowledge of the local ecology and of the long-term social and environmental impacts of their activities. Now, a growing body of scientific research confirms this belief.[27]

Community-based management systems are neither perfect nor foolproof. As in any form of social organization, competing interests abound and disagreements often ensue. But a distinctive feature of an authentic community-based system is the institutionalization of conflict-management mechanisms. These have evolved over the years from underlying and supportive social and cultural mores. In general, the threat of religious sanction or social ostracism undergirds rules for using and protecting forest resources. The enforcers tend to be resource bosses, appointed committees, and rotating forest guards who regularly monitor resources and extractive activities. In some cases, ritual activities in one community reinforce similar enforcement mechanisms in neighboring communities.[28]

Community-based management does not always maximize forest resources, but these systems usually stabilize when they sustain an appropriate population. Above all, the systems themselves and the property rights they are based upon evolve—as few state-managed systems seem to—in response to changes in social and environmental conditions, including relationships with nearby communities and with conservationists, the military, commercial buyers, and other outsiders. Moreover, when a resource becomes scarce, communities often draw on the base with more moderation.

Box 4. Another Viewpoint: Who Carries the Biggest Stick?

The seeds of current resource degradation were planted in the late 18th century when resource harvesting became the norm because resources seemed limitless. This practice became embedded in the colonial culture and the attitudes of the ruling elites—parts of which live on.

Property rights are not contingent on state grants or documentation. Nor should they be. But what are they based on? Community-based property rights are as legitimate as state-sanctioned individual ones, and rights of any sort carry correlated duties. Often, rights require defending. But how and by whom? Good will is too often insufficient. Moral reasoning too has been known to fail. Duties thus arise from the credible threat of an authority system. Without one, no rights exist.

Coherent empirical rights, unfortunately, require compulsion, which must originate with an authority. Often, the necessary and sufficient compulsion resides at the community level. Indeed, the local community is an authority system with a legal personality that can undertake binding contracts with its members and can oversee contracts promulgated between legal personalities within its domain.

But what happens when forces from beyond the domain of the local community come to bear on contractual relations embedded within it? For instance, an authority system well-geared to enforcing contracts within its domain is likely to find itself powerless before logging concessionaires operating with the blessings of Jakarta or Manila. There is a boundary problem here.[a]

The local community can quite well be sovereign (have legal competence and legitimacy) within its acknowledged territory. But at the boundary—where its domain butts up against that of yet another sovereign local community—legal incoherence may reign.

For example, what happens if loggers move in on one or both domains? Or if a member of a neighboring domain intrudes on another? Without some higher authority, the strongest survive at any cost—whether through anarchy or repression. Who wins in a state of nature? The party with the biggest stick. Do we want boundary disputes resolved on the basis of who carries it?

Ultimately, a unit of larger scale may be implicated in disputes at the boundary of quite legitimate—and in most instances quite adequate—local communities. Unless and until an authority system at

Box 4. (continued)

some higher level than the local community (and its authority system) is available to recognize the external legitimacy of community-based resource management regimes, their beneficence is irrelevant because of their impotence. When the chips are down, those at the center are going to coerce local communities to get resources.

With no suprastate authority, it is unrealistic to expect that elites will suddenly husband natural resources and look kindly on the people who depend on them, especially since elites regard the reckless harvesting of natural resources as a birthright. For this reason alone, community rights management schemes must be backed up by coercion. Otherwise, individuals within a community may be quite well protected against a predatory cousin on the next ridge, but totally exposed to comparable loggers from Manila.

Community-based and local resource management are both promising and, often, effective. But until nation-states grant legitimacy and protection to such regimes, they will not catch on or advance. Higher-level recognition and protection of the community-based property arrangements (and the local capacity to govern resource use) are needed along with local coherent structures of rules and authority.

While this grant or recognition is both rare and bureaucratically cumbersome, effective resource management at the local level is impossible without it. These arrangements need to become both less unusual and less challenging. The sample contracts in Appendices A and B show how. Private community rights seem a contradiction in terms. Are they common property regimes wherein members of the community hold rights and duties with respect to other members with regard to certain natural resources? The members of the community are joint owners of something, or owners in common, but private? Common property regimes may correctly be defined as private property for the group, but the private property language suggests complete alienability and managerial discretion among all of the co-owners. If so, then governments and local communities may balk at accepting this idea. The historical commons was not a confusing concept. Why it should be so now is a mystery—especially given the prevalence of condominiums, time-share apartments, swimming clubs, country clubs, and the like.

> **Box 4.** (continued)
>
> **Notes**
> a. Daniel W. Bromley, *Environment and Economy: Property Rights and Public Policy* (Oxford: Blackwell, 1991).
>
> *Source:* Personal communication with Daniel W. Bromley, Anderson-Bascom Professor, University of Wisconsin at Madison.

Where survival is not at stake, restricted usufruct rights and community-based enforcement mechanisms usually have this effect.

Despite the incentives to adapt, some communities fail and forest resources become degraded. Why other communities faced with similar circumstances in the same geographical area prove able to make productive changes is not well documented, but some degree of tenurial security clearly plays an important role.[29]

After analyzing several case studies of community-based property rights, Elinor Ostrom found that the most successful systems followed eight design principles:

1. The boundaries of the user-groups and the resources are well-defined.
2. Use rules are locally specific and appropriate.
3. Rule modification is participatory and locally managed.
4. Users monitor compliance.
5. Users determine sanctions.
6. Low-cost conflict resolution mechanisms are available.
7. Local rights and institutions are independent of external governments.
8. In some situations, an inclusive federal system overlaps the local system.[30]

Empirical evidence from around the world shows that farmers and other resource users are highly skeptical of government programs that provide them with only limited tenure rights in local forests.[31] But other than rejecting the package offered to them by powerful forest departments, forest dwellers often have little practical choice in the matter. Even the more progressive forestry programs in the region, such as India's joint forest-management program and Nepal's "handing it over" policy, stipulate that community forest users' groups have only usufruct rights of management over the trees—not ownership rights to the land.

No matter what tenurial arrangement exists between the state and local peoples, the success of community-based management programs ultimately depends on the extent and security of those rights that are recognized or granted. For this reason, tenurial control over trees or management rights of harvest are limited in scope. Not surprisingly, when only limited rights are bestowed, acceptance of the management duties that government policy-makers seek to devolve are often agreed to with limited commitment.

In addition, contradictions between oral customary laws and the written codes, regulations, and statutes related to tenurial rights to forest and other natural resources are exacerbated by conflicting interests among local peoples and government authorities. Such conflicts make both parties more reluctant to work out equitable arrangements for managing forests for sustainable use and conservation.

II.
HISTORICAL OVERVIEW: COLONIAL PATTERNS OF FOREST MANAGEMENT

Although recent improvements in carbon-dating technology have revised the age of the *pithecanthropus erectus* remains found near Travil on Java (hence, the name "Java man"), from 1.2 to 1.8 million years[32] some anthropologists speculate that the year-round growing season and the extensive natural resource base delayed the development of large, settled societies in Asia and the Pacific. With abundant food, water, and building materials, early inhabitants had little need to structure communities extensively either to produce goods collectively or for defense.[33]

According to this theory, the development of non-migratory agriculture, especially wet-rice cultivation and the sophisticated, labor-intensive irrigation systems it requires, prompted the formation of sedentary societies. The lure of easy gathering and regular harvests induced once-itinerant cultivators and hunter-gatherers to settle in close proximity and establish more elaborate social structures.[34] Artifacts unearthed at Spirit Cave in northwestern Thailand indicate that settled cultivation was under way as early as 10,000 b.c.[35]

Over time, broad regularly-inundated river valleys that had once been lightly populated became the home of thriving—and often complex—societies based on wet rice culture. Free from the need to prepare for months when game and produce are scarce, these civilizations developed highly sophisticated cultures, rich in arts and crafts, that sometimes culminated in the construction of magnificent temples.[36] Those with access to sea channels also engaged in mutually enriching trade.

Most upland cultures tend to be less complex than their lowland counterparts. Left to their own devices, forest communities developed sustainable agricultural and forestry practices tailored to the various challenges posed by upland terrains and soils. Many survive today in only slightly modified form. Because heavy rainfall induces erosion and leaching on upland tropical soils and because vital nutrients drain away in perpetual growing seasons, many upland forest farmers move frequently. In many cases, shifting cultivation is the only viable agricultural system.

The Colonial Foundations

Beginning in the early 1500s, European seafaring nations (especially Portugal, the Netherlands, and England) tried to decrease their reliance on African and Arab traders by forging trading links with the East. At first, European merchants mainly sought what they could extract as material exports for quick profits, teak from India, spices from Indonesia, tin from Thailand, and copra from the Philippines, for instance. Commercial cartels, such as The East India Company (Britain) and the Vereenigde Oostindische Compagnie (the Netherlands), established trade alliances with some of the prosperous lowland kingdoms of South and Southeast Asia. How they were received depended upon both the inclination of colonial officials and the indigenous populations and their leaders, some of whom at first welcomed foreigners. Where local resistance was minimal or non-existent, the Europeans dictated the terms of commerce, limited only by practical considerations, such as how much they could get out of native populations before cooperation, and thus productivity, ceased.

For the better part of 300 years, the colonial history of South and Southeast Asia was determined by the nature of such commercial enterprises. Unlike in the Americas, there were no great migrations of European settlers to Asia that would overwhelm local cultures or devalue collaboration with native populations. In pursuit of a steady supply of spices, wood, fruits, and nuts, Europeans recruited native leaders as junior partners. In return for securing labor and providing logistical expertise, these leaders received highly valued European manufactured goods and many assumed official positions in colonial governments. Whatever benefit this intercontinental trade had for Asian societies was minute compared to the personal aggrandizement of European entrepreneurs and their Asian collaborators.

Providing for European consumers was an acknowledged prerogative of the colonial administration and investing entrepreneurs. Meanwhile, Asian suppliers, newly introduced to cash economies and an assortment of goods they had never before enjoyed, soon developed new tastes and appetites for goods manufactured in Europe. In this interplay, forest resources provided them with a means of exchange.

The Industrial Revolution heightened European demand for Asian and Pacific resources—first as the raw materials of industry and then as consumer goods for an expanding and increasingly prosperous middle class. Together, these demands well exceeded European production capacities. Most Asian and Pacific agricultural and forest products—among them, rubber, sugar cane, coffee, cotton, tea, and quinine—could not be grown in temperate climates. Others, such as timber, couldn't be met by degraded European forests.[37]

In their rush to appropriate for themselves (and pre-empt their European rivals), colonial nations claimed sovereignty over territories far in excess of what their administrative staffs could manage. As in Africa and the Americas, disparate indigenous cultures often found themselves joined geopolitically under the same European aegis. To deal with their extensive new territories, Europeans tried to impose Western notions of sovereignty and property rights, approaches particularly intrusive in these predominately oral and communal societies.

In some areas, the exponential growth of plantation agriculture and commercial logging, both of which require large tracts of land, dramatically altered pre-colonial societies. Securing colonial legal access often required usurping traditional tenurial rights. Having legally appropriated land and forest resources, the colonial states granted extensive concessions without regard for the needs, or often even the survival, of forest dependent communities. When obvious overexploitation ensued, colonial extractors dismissed the destruction. Based on their own observations of rapid tropical growth, some no doubt believed that nature would replenish what they took away. Others didn't care.

Colonial entrepreneurs used their military advantage to commandeer what they could not easily acquire through negotiation or fraud. European systems of resource ownership and management encouraged colonial officials to ignore the predominantly oral nature of traditional ownership regimes. Without written documentation to support their claims, indigenous communities and individuals were at a pronounced disadvantage under colonial regimes. Centuries of established and functional tenurial systems were usurped, often with the single stroke of a colonial administrator's pen. With certain notable exceptions—such as the Indian Rebellion of 1857—once the European colonialists had established their territorial claims, few major clashes followed.

Although they claimed sovereignty over huge expanses of land, the colonial powers were primarily interested in what they considered the productive parts of those territories. For this reason, other areas continued to be managed by local communities in accordance with traditional practices until they came within range of the inexorably expanding commercial activities.

Like other European traders, British entrepreneurs and administrators initially recognized and respected indigenous legal systems of South Asia. The Napoleonic conflict, however, which pitted Britain against its main economic rival, the Netherlands, provided an impetus to experiment with wholesale legal appropriation. In 1811, a much superior military force under the command of Thomas S. Raffles invaded and easily defeated Dutch settlers on Java. As the new British authority, Lt. Governor Raffles proclaimed that "the proprietary rights to land in Java were vested in the sovereign and thus in the European Government as the successor of the Javanese sovereigns."[38] The sweeping usurpation of community-based property rights in Asia had begun.

Sri Lanka

Prior to the arrival of the Europeans, the Sinhalese kings ruled what is today the nation of Sri Lanka through a complex system of tenurial rights. In return for their service as soldiers, artisans, or farmers, the monarch bestowed upon his subjects the legal rights to parcels of land. Under this system, every Sri Lankan male had the right to a parcel of land, which he could use or manage as he saw fit, provided he served the king as required.

Map of Sri Lanka

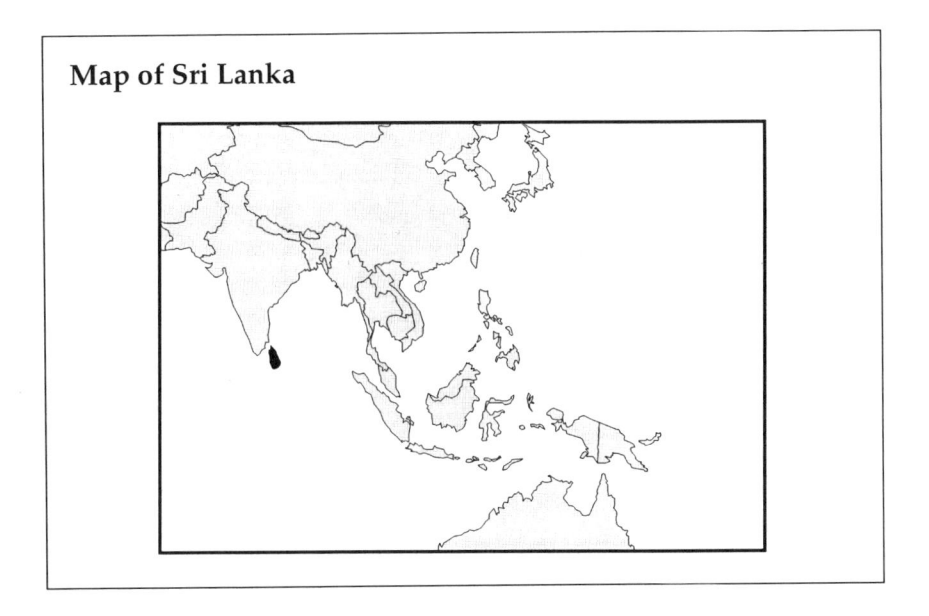

The colonial marginalization of Sinhalese people commenced in the early 16th century, when the Portuguese arrived in search of cinnamon and other spices. Portuguese rule, limited to coastal areas, gave way to Dutch rule, in 1658. Although they acknowledged traditional service tenure, the Dutch promoted the documentary registration of claims, called thombos, of all such land held in their areas of control. In 1796, the British ejected the Dutch and with the signing of the Kandyan Convention in 1815, the entire island came under British colonial rule. Shortly after assuming control, the British attempted to replace traditional service tenures with "adequate pay."[39] Tenure holders protested, and eight years later the British restored service tenures.

The conflict between the British and forest-dependent peoples was primarily economic. At issue was coffee, the East India Company's most profitable commodity. With demand at record highs, expanding coffee plantations encroached into areas used for swidden agriculture *(chena)*. Denounced by the Dutch as a "robber economy," *chena* drew similar protests from British planters chafing because they could not expand their coffee plantations.

35

In 1840, the British Colonial Administration ruled in favor of the planters by promulgating the Crown Lands (Encroachment) Ordinance which abrogated undocumented community-based property rights and declared that all "forests, waste, unoccupied, or uncultivated land" were vested in the Crown.[40] Fallow *chena* lands were deemed "unoccupied" and "uncultivated," and the crown quickly made them available to the cartel's planters. A century and a half later, this ordinance remains the legal foundation for most recognized property rights in modern Sri Lanka.

India

The Ceylonese solution soon extended to India, the jewel in England's colonial crown. Historical records show that India's forests were both rich and extensive, even though they had supported large populations of people and livestock for thousands of years. Over the centuries, forest management systems ranging from the simple to the complex evolved throughout the subcontinent. While variations from place to place were great, as a rule, these systems were local in origin. Governing forests was typically a community

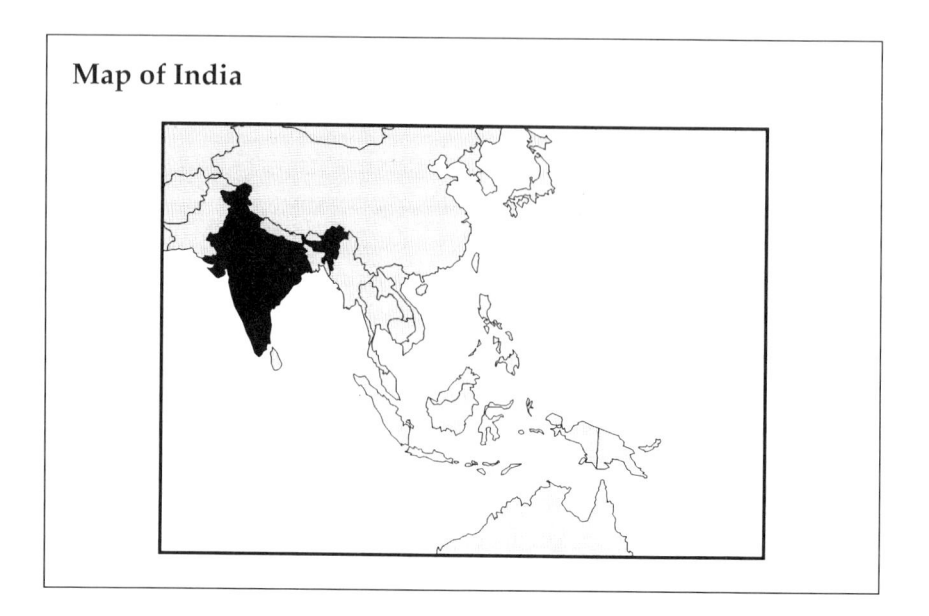

Map of India

prerogative, one seldom challenged by the maharajahs, princes, and other authorities.

For the first century or so after Clive's conquest of Bengal in 1757, most community-based systems survived, and the Forest Act of 1865 stipulated that it would "not abridge or affect any existing rights of individuals or communities." But when the railway boom began, the demand for wood, especially teak, skyrocketed and the Forest Act of 1878 signed by the Governor General of India was a strikingly different type of law. The law (most of which would be reiterated in the Forest Act of 1927, a law still in effect nearly seventy years later) paved the way for the state to assert control over most Indian forests.

As the self-proclaimed "legal inheritors" of the sovereignty of conquered maharajahs and other local rulers, the British essentially granted themselves authority to appropriate whatever they wanted. They considered the colonial state the rightful owner of most "wastelands," a term applied to all lands not permanently settled, including forests. These areas were available for annexation, regardless of competing community rights.

Under the Forest Act of 1878, the colonial government could demarcate and establish state-owned reserves and protected forests. The government realized that it would not be feasible to simply eliminate all customary uses of forest resources, so the Act established procedures for recognizing certain pre-existing rights. These often cumbersome procedures gave forestry officials wide discretion. As a result, the degree of community usage that was tolerated tended to depend on the value of the resources to outsiders and the capacity of communities to resist territorial encroachment. A careful assessment of local customs and needs, or the carrying capacity of the forest, rarely entered into the decision.

In practice, where local forest usage was allowed under the Forest Act, the government usually proffered little legal protection. Use was instead deemed to be a "privilege" granted by a benevolent sovereign—who could, of course, easily reduce, revoke, or revise it. The working assumption was that whatever rights or access communities had to forest resources ultimately depended on the goodwill of the colonial regime. Above all, government forest policy denied the legitimacy of community-based rules and institutions.

Over the ensuing decades, "Forest Privilege Codes" were compiled. These specified which tribes, castes, villages, and other social organizations had access privileges to forest resources for grazing or gathering. While the government aimed "to concede liberal privileges...to communities which are reported to enjoy them," official documents made it clear that this was done as a "matter of favor and not of right." Such favors, of course, were "subject to withdrawal at any time."

Only in remote areas outside the colonial pale did community systems continue to operate without serious interference. Everywhere else, colonial authorities seriously disrupted local institutions and management practices, but substituted no effective measures. Gradually, on more and more of India's forests the British regime prevented community-based institutions from functioning. Nor did it put viable alternatives into place. Skirmishes and outright rebellions became common as local communities, facing the loss of their traditional resource base, fought to retain historical prerogatives. But British firepower overwhelmed these determined but poorly-equipped community groups, and India's forests fell under the nominal, sporadic control of colonial forest departments.

Nepal

Because of its remote mountainous setting, Nepal remained essentially immune to the British colonial administration. Forced to accept British authority—but not occupation—by the Treaty of Sugouli in 1816, the ruling Shah dynasty retreated into isolation. In 1846, a corrupt oligarchy assumed hegemony over what had been isolated and self-sufficient ethnic groups. The Rana premiers, as they came to be known, secured their power through an effective administrative system: repressive new legislation, rigorous tax collection, and forced labor. To expand their tax base, the Rana rulers promoted the conversion of forests to farms, especially in the Tarai and the sparsely populated southern lowlands.

The Ranas' reclusive feudalism reigned in Nepal until the early 1950s. Most of the ethnically diverse Nepali people were subjugated to elites from favored castes and ethnic groups. As

> **Map of Nepal**

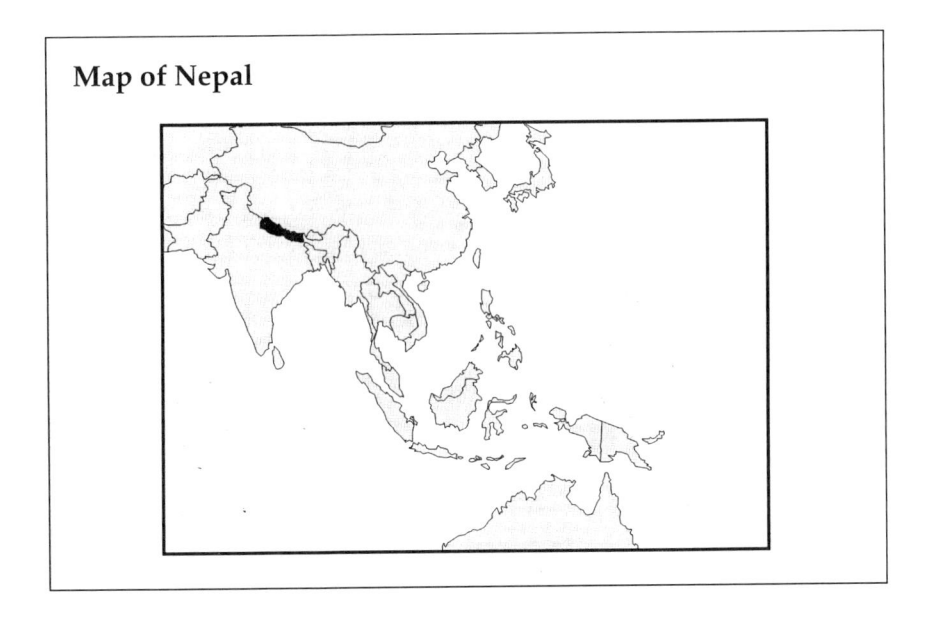

late as mid-century, approximately one third of the forests were managed under birta tenure whereby the state granted rights to forest resources to private individuals tax-free on a hereditary basis.[41] A full quarter of Nepal's forests remained under Rana family control.[42]

Although abusive and expropriative, the Rana regime never had the administrative wherewithal or the financial incentive to lead Nepal down a destructively extractive path. For most of Nepal's indigenous peoples, the ruling oligarchy's reach was insufficient to disrupt historical patterns of community-based forest management. In addition, in most of the country's commercially viable forests, malaria was rampant.

Since Nepal was never—like India and Sri Lanka were—subjected to intensive colonial extractive activities, the resources of the semiautonomous kingdom were left to the devices of the ruling Rana oligarchy, which used them mostly to maintain their power and wealth rather than to maximize economic gain. It would not be until the overthrow of the Rana regime in the early 1950s that Nepal would enter the modern world.

Indonesia

The British were not alone in usurping customary rights and establishing expansive claims of state ownership. Upon re-acquiring Indonesia in 1816, the Dutch —who had never systematically addressed the issue of traditional rights—let Raffles' Java declaration stand, merely adding that indigenous rights not "interfering" with European sovereignty would continue to be recognized.

Over the next 50 years, that "interference" threshold would be delineated by the now-familiar dynamic between indigenous management systems and plantation agriculture. In 1830, a new governor-general imposed an agricultural program that came to be known as the Culture System, which essentially forced Javanese peasants to pay their rents in government-dictated export crops. Originally, the peasants had to plant one fifth of their land according to the colonial mandate, but that requirement was soon upped. In some places, peasants were so hard-pressed to meet their quotas, which some corrupt officials increased, that they had to neglect their subsistence crops. During the mid 1840s, famines induced by the Culture System racked central Java and fomented popular agitation.

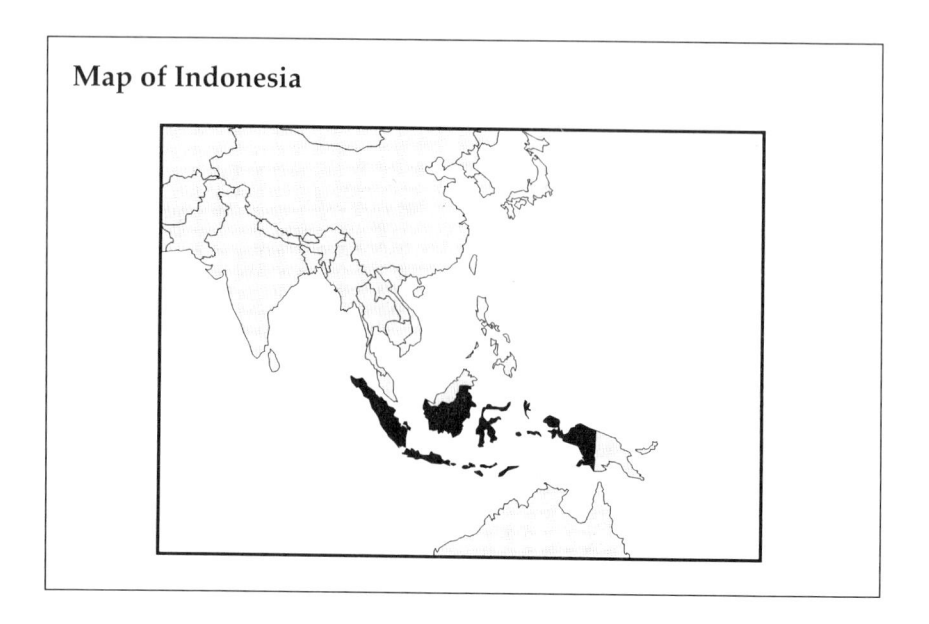

Map of Indonesia

By the 1860s, unprecedented increases in Java's local population brought shifting agriculture into protracted conflict with the expanded and lucrative coffee trade. Predictably, the interests of colonial commerce prevailed in the form of the Agrarian Act of 1870. Drafted to counter the Culture System, this Act enabled private capitalists to lease lands from the colonial government for up to 75 years and prevented Indonesians from selling their land to non-Indonesians (an attempt to preclude famine by assuring that Indonesians would retain control over enough land to feed themselves).

By stipulating that customary property rights, known in Indonesia as adat, would be recognized only on continually cultivated lands, the Agrarian Act undermined previous accommodations between colonial and indigenous forest management on the Inner Islands of Java and Madura. Officially authorized uses of the forest took precedence over all traditional practices. The Dutch colonial government could now do anything it wanted with the land under its legal control. As colonial commerce spread into the Outer Islands, the Act was eventually expanded to cover them as well.

The Philippines

Unlike their counterparts from the Netherlands and Britain, Spanish administrators recognized two kinds of private property rights during the first 350 years of their rule in the Philippines: those held by custom and those held by the Crown. Customary rights were predicated on usage and possession, while portions of the royal domain, or terrenos realengos, were bestowed by the Crown and its authorized subordinates to colonial entrepreneurs. Soon after the first Governor General and his entourage arrived, royal grants of these crown lands established private estates for "deserving" Spanish citizens.[43]

Debate over the legal basis of Spain's sovereignty in its far-flung empire in the Philippines and the Americas influenced official attitudes toward the Crown's ownership of land and other natural resources. The debate was prompted in part by reports of greed and the brutality being inflicted by Spanish colonists on indigenous Americans. Initially hesitant, King Philip II resolved that a similar fate would not befall the Philippine natives, and made an

Map of The Philippines

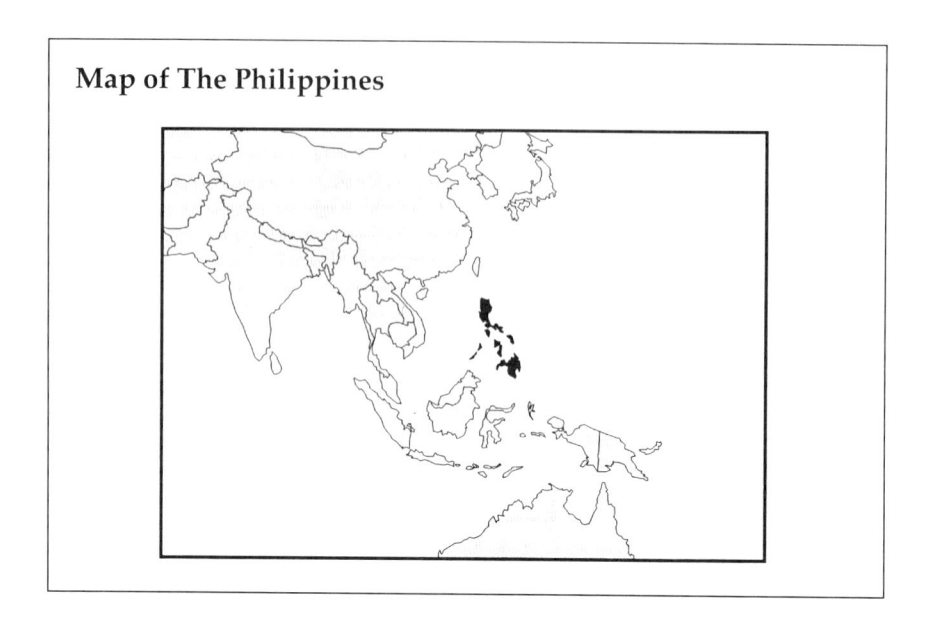

"irrevocable commitment of the Spanish colonial policy" to treat "natives as `new Christians,' [who] merited some effective guarantees of their property rights."[44] The various laws promulgated to promote these guarantees, many of which also applied to non-Christians, allowed land to be apportioned among the Philippine colonists, but did not allow them to "occupy or take possession of any private property of the Indians."[45]

In theory, the royal decrees provided potentially important recognition of community-based rights. In practice, however, the decrees were often disobeyed and ignored. Although colonial authorities documented and registered individual land rights to religious orders, institutions, and corporations (legal entities treated as "individuals"), community-based tenurial rights to ancestral domains were seen as non-recognizable abstractions. Indigenous communities, thus, had no documentary existence and were unable to secure recognition of their rights. Meanwhile, Spanish colonials, as well as native and Chinese *mestizo* elites, regularly usurped community-based rights.

The Spanish colonial government was continually bedeviled by confusion and unrest over the nature and extent of land rights.

The legal significance of land registration, for example, was never conclusively resolved. Land laws consisted of "numberless single decrees forming a casuistical, disconnected, complicated and confused mass."[46] Further complicating the situation, the Spanish administration failed to keep systematic records.[47]

Most ancestral domains in the Philippines, like those in other Asian colonies, remained beyond colonial control. The farther from Manila, Cebu, or other colonial centers, or the lower the perceived value of the land, the greater the likelihood that indigenous patterns of resource allocation would remain intact. But the security provided by distance or isolation lasted only as long as the forces of technology, population growth, and material acquisitiveness stayed at bay. Under the impetus of lucrative plantation agriculture, especially sugar cane and tobacco, colonial rule spread throughout the islands.

In the late 1820s, Manuel Bernaldez, a high-ranking colonial official who had spent 17 years in the Philippines, noted that the Indians of the villages typically provided proof of their customary property rights by evidence of tradition and the depositions of witnesses. Claiming that customary rights prompted controversy and litigation, Bernaldez called for the Crown to oblige all the villages and private individual landowners to acquire official documentation of their ownership.[48] Indigenous peoples who didn't secure official documentation would not have their ancestral-domain rights recognized and would become squatters on Crown lands.

Seventy years later, colonial administrators in Manila resorted to Bernaldez's ploy in a last-ditch attempt to address the widespread resentment caused by the spread of plantation agriculture and confusion over the documented-property regime. The preamble of the Royal Decree of February 13, 1894 (known as the "Maura Act") declared that it would "insure to the natives, in the future, whenever it may be possible, the necessary land for cultivation, in accordance with traditional usages." Article 4, however, revealed a different purpose, providing that undocumented property rights would revert to the colonial state. Those with land-title applications pending had one year to document their claims. No extensions were allowed, and any titles issued after April 17, 1895, would have "no force and effect."

The Maura Act highlighted the colonial regime's insensitivity to the plight and potential of the colony's poor rural majority. By empowering colonial officials to deny legal recognition of community-based property rights, the Maura Act reneged on Spain's three-centuries-old (albeit largely ignored) commitment to respect such traditions, thus disenfranchising several million rural farmers.

To the great majority of the rural poor, the very idea of a documented land title was foreign and the Maura Law was incomprehensible. Most of the few who acquired legal titles had collaborated with and prospered under the colonial regime, and these so-called caciques often laid claim to more land than they had a legitimate right to. In many cases, peasants who had been using land for generations, but had not known or cared about documentary titles, were suddenly confronted by influential people invoking colonial law and claiming their land. Many people surprised by this legal change were forced to flee their ancestral areas or became tenants.[49]

Two years after the Maura Law was enacted, the first revolution against colonial rule in Southeast Asia erupted in the Philippines, partly because of inequitable allocation of legal rights to natural resources. In 1898, before the revolution had played itself out, the United States acquired the Philippines as a result of the Spanish-American War.[50] Despite strong anti-imperialist sentiment in the U.S. Congress and the popular press, the new colonial administration, encouraged by domestic agricultural interests, maintained the inequities that resulted from the Maura Act. A fire in Manila in 1897 that destroyed the main repository of documents pertaining to land titles and claims undermined what few legal rights had been recognized.

To justify and perpetuate the expropriations based on the Maura Act of 1894—and hence their own holdings—the U.S. colonial government devised and promoted a legal myth now known as the "Regalian Doctrine" (from the adjective "regal"). According to this fabrication, Ferdinand Magellan appropriated every Filipino forebears' sovereignty and property rights when he planted a cross on a small island in the middle of the archipelago in 1521. At that moment, every native in the still- unexplored (not to mention unconquered, as Magellan would soon attest with his life) archipelago technically became a squatter, bereft of legal rights to land or other natural resources.

The mythical Regalian Doctrine provided the new colonial regime with a convenient legal pretext for claiming ownership of more than 90 percent of the Philippines' total land mass. It likewise nurtured the largely unrealized hope of senior U.S. colonial officials who believed that they could lure U.S. corporations—especially sugar-cane-growing enterprises—to the Philippines by providing them with legal rights over large tracts of fertile land.[51] A ruling by the U.S. Supreme Court in 1909 which refuted the Regalian Doctrine *(see Box 5)*, meanwhile, was essentially ignored by the Manila-based regime.

Box 5. The U.S. Supreme Court v. the Regalian Doctrine

The Regalian Doctrine was legally refuted in a 1909 U. S. Supreme Court decision, *Cariño v. the Insular Government*. Written by Oliver Wendell Holmes for a unanimous court, this decision affirmed that land occupied in the Philippines since time immemorial was never legally public land. Holmes emphasized that even if Spain refused to recognize the undocumented community-based property rights of indigenous occupants, it did "not follow that, in the view of the United States, [they] had lost all rights and [were] mere trespasser[s]." On the other hand, Holmes went on to chasten those who interpreted the Maura Law as being "the confiscation of a right" by opining that the Maura Law merely "[w]ithdrew the privilege to register rights."

Holmes considered the Regalian Doctrine repugnant, noting that the argument "seems to amount to a denial of native titles...for the want of ceremonies which the Spaniards would not have permitted and had not the power to enforce." He was shocked that the U.S. government:

> was ready to declare that "any person" did not embrace the inhabitants of [Cariño's home province of] Benguet, or that it meant by "property" only that which had become such by ceremonies of which presumably a large part of the inhabitants never had heard, and that it proposed to treat as public land what they,

> **Box 5.** (continued)
>
> by native custom and by long association—one of the profoundest factors in human thought—regarded as their own.[a]
>
> The Cariño decision has never been overruled or reversed, and it remains good law in the Philippines. Even so, U.S. colonial officials and their successors in the Philippine Republic have ignored it in favor of the historically and legally flawed Regalian Doctrine for more than 80 years.[b]
>
> **Notes**
> a. United States Report, 212:449.
> b. See generally Dante B. Gatmaytan, "Ancestral Domain Recognition in the Philippines: Trends in Jurisprudence and Legislation," *Philippine Natural Resources Law Journal* 5:43–90, 1992.

Thailand

Although their country was never actually occupied by the Europeans, Thai rulers adopted the mentality of the colonial powers when it came to managing forests. Like European colonial powers in neighboring regions, Thailand (called Siam until 1939), profited from exploiting its timber resources. A commercially active and relatively centralized state, Thai leaders early on saw the opportunity to trade forest resources, especially high-quality teak, with Britain and other countries for manufactured goods. In this regard, Thailand took the path its neighbors would take nearly a century later after they became independent.

Commercial forestry in Thailand began in the mid-19th century and continued to expand as roads and railways were built. The monarchy in Bangkok became alarmed when local princely states, working with British foresters across the border in Burma,[52] commercially exploited the most productive teak forests. In these transactions nothing came into the royal coffers, and such streaks of independence chafed. During the last decade of the nineteenth

> **Map of Thailand**

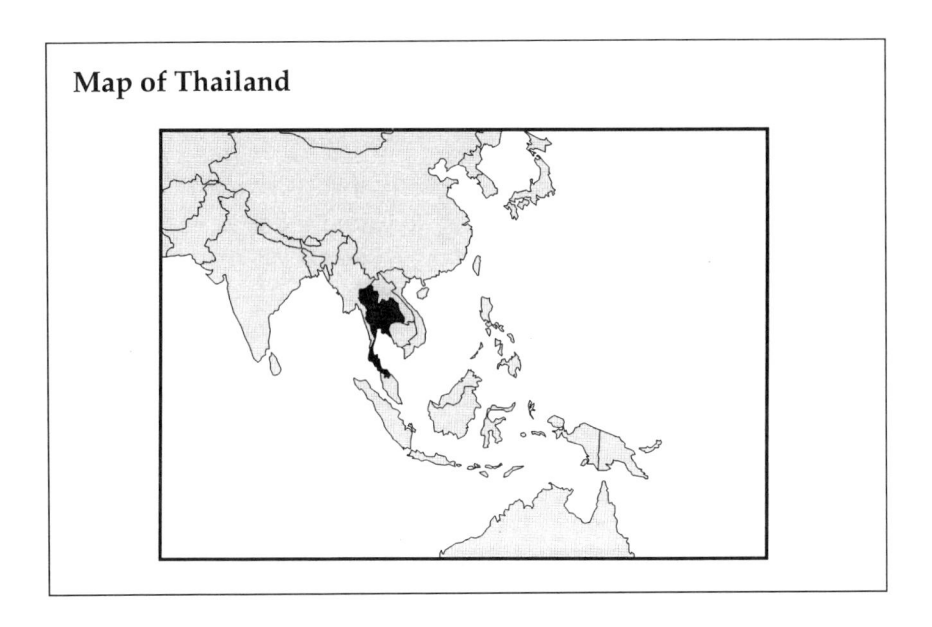

century, King Chulalongkorn ended these partnerships by proclaiming the monarchy's legal ownership of all land.[53]

Since centralized control requires a supporting bureaucracy and legal system, numerous laws were enacted to ensure that the state profited from the teak trade of the late 1890s. In 1896, the Royal Forestry Department was established. Soon after came enactment of the Forest Protection Act, the Teak Trees Protection Act, a law prohibiting the unauthorized marketing of timber, and another outlawing teak extraction unless duties and royalties were paid.[54]

Initially, as in the Philippines, Thailand's assertion of legal control over forest resources did not keep most local farmers from acquiring property rights pursuant to customary norms requiring *de facto* occupancy and cultivation. In 1901, however, King Chulalongkorn formally introduced the Western concept of documented individual private ownership in a new law that also distinguished "factual occupancy from ownership, and...created a system in which no protection [was] given to occupancy but only to ownership."[55]

The 1901 law resulted in both confusion and injustice. Bangkok elites took advantage of their connections and proximity to the central government to procure ownership documents for land long

47

cultivated by rural farmers ignorant of the new law and, hence, of the need for documentation. For several decades the sheer size of the kingdom's arable land area, its low population density, and the customary mobility of Thai farmers mitigated social discord. But simmering disputes ignited when the Forest Act of 1941 redefined forest as "land which has not been acquired by any person under the land law." (Section 4(1)). Farming in such areas denominated as the *Pah Sa-nguan* (roughly, public forest land) was legal only if it followed stringent dictates from the Royal Forestry Department. Not surprisingly, most existing community-based agroforestry and forest management systems violated these rules.

From the perspective of forest preservation, the most detrimental aspect of the 1941 legislation was its implication that the *Pah Sa-nguan* could be diminished as farmers established or were granted titles over "unclaimed" forest land. The functionally negative definition created incentives for entrepreneurs and landless farmers to migrate into previously forested areas and establish claims. In the wake of World War II, poverty, land speculation, and population pressures generated a surge of legal claims over the nation's forest lands, particularly in the sparsely-populated northeast.

The Rise of Asian Elites

An inevitable consequence of centuries of lucrative trade in minerals, timber, exotic agricultural crops, drugs, and spices, was that increasingly powerful groups of privileged Asian elites were formed. At first, only aristocratic or otherwise politically connected settlers and entrepreneurs profited from the European-controlled colonial commerce. But, over time, traders and community leaders—generally Chinese or from dominant ethnic groups—were absorbed into the expanding circle of wealth. Slowly, these favored few grew more wealthy (especially in relation to other natives) and coalesced into local oligarchies. Like European colonials, Asian oligarchies flourished primarily at the expense of the rural poor by exploiting their resources and land and ignoring or usurping their community-based rights.

The progression from subordinate to junior partner and, ultimately to sovereign nation-states was enhanced by a steady increase in volumes of trade and profit. By the early 20th century, advances in technology and transportation made extraction and plantation enterprises highly lucrative. While agricultural tycoons expanded their holdings, generally at the expense of nearby smallholders, timber concessionaires relocated their operations from degraded forest to unexploited tract. Frequently, migrations of scattered populations of displaced indigenous peoples resulted.

Given abundant forest holdings and steady and growing demand from the colonizing countries, the concession system continued to prosper until the worldwide depression of the 1930s. But before the depression had run its course, World War II erupted and the Japanese army occupied many parts of mainland and insular Southeast Asia. To an area already beset by declines in revenues and the deterioration of infrastructure, the War brought widespread social and economic upheaval. In its wake went 400 years of colonialism.

III.
Contemporary Overview: The Legacies of State Ownership

World War II hastened the demise of the colonial system in South and Southeast Asia. Oppressive occupation by the Japanese military transformed predominantly intellectual independence movements into direct action. Under European domination, narrow but powerful cartels of indigenous elites had flourished, but the war's cessation of European trade spurred many to join organized resistance movements and lay the foundations of the elite/military alliances that continue to dominate some countries in the region.

After the war, financially strapped and physically decimated European powers were hard pressed to simply rebuild themselves, much less to attend to distant Asian colonies. Pleas to reclaim colonies that could not be protected fell on unsympathetic ears. Although some European powers, particularly Britain and France, would cling to their pre-war empires for as long as possible, independence was a foregone conclusion. The only questions were when and under what terms. By 1950, those questions had been largely answered in Asia—with varying degrees of bloodshed, bitterness, and even some goodwill.

The New Colonialists

Even though most Asian elites protested colonialism, after independence they and their successors preserved most of the legal inequalities and inertia of the colonial systems from which they had benefitted. For the most part, the colonial states simply converted into nation states with virtually identical bureaucracies and many of the same officials, although in some countries the military assumed greater prominence.

Retained in spirit, and largely in letter, were the inequitable colonial legal systems overlaid with progressive-sounding constitutions. Foremost among these—as far as community-based forest management is concerned—were colonial/national laws regarding the ownership and use of natural resources. Indeed, in many respects, existing national laws are more hostile to the rights, claims, and aspirations of forest dependent peoples than were their colonial predecessors. The nationalization of forest areas, meanwhile, has had disastrous results, especially in areas under community-based management.

Indonesia

Nowhere in Southeast Asia has the colonial mentality—favoring centralized retention of legal power and authority over local resources and management practices—remained more pervasive than in Indonesia. The size of the nation's forest lands and their immense profit-making potential undoubtedly help perpetuate the state's all-inclusive claim of ownership over forest resources.

The New Order government that emerged in 1965 after bitter civil strife has systematically limited the rights of local communities, non-governmental organizations, labor, and other social sectors to organize themselves for either economic development or political participation. In addition, neither the legislative nor the judicial branch provides effective checks on the ruling oligarchy's power. Some nascent, hopeful developments aside, community-based forest management continues to be under-utilized.

Under the Indonesian constitution, the national government retains authority and responsibility for those "branches of production, which are important for the State and which affect the lives of most people." Invoking this authority, the Basic Forestry Law of 1967 empowers the Ministry of Forestry to "determine and regulate legal relations between individuals or corporate bodies and forests, and deal with legal activities related to forests." The power extends over roughly 143 million hectares now classified as public forest land.

These forests also support the wide-ranging authorized and unauthorized activities of large timber companies, migrant cultivators, small-scale gold-panners and others. Since none of them holds secure rights to forest resources or has any way to exclude others, especially in remote areas, the resulting *de facto* "open access" situation provides compelling opportunities to deforest and degrade.[56]

Some who stake claims, especially wealthy and technically sophisticated logging firms and other concession-holders, receive the state's imprimatur, which includes legal rights to exploit particular forest territories and resources, and the state stands ready to enforce their rights. Forest dwellers without state support can appeal only to community-based rights, which are often ignored outside the community, and attempt to defy the government-sanctioned intrusions.

Indonesia's commercial logging boom was precipitated by the implementing regulations of the Basic Forestry Law and the Law on Foreign Investment (both passed in 1967). In their wake, the traditional adat tenurial rights of millions of forest-dwelling and forest-dependent people in Indonesia's Outer Islands have been steadily subordinated to the profits of a relatively small number of commercial firms and state enterprises or, for conservation purposes, to the Ministry of Forestry. The "legal" disenfranchisement of forest communities is reflected in government policies that divide forest-dependent peoples into two groups. The *perambah hutan* or "forest squatters" are recent arrivals, while the *masyarakat terasing*, or "isolated communities," are the traditional forest-dwellers with long tenure on the land who—according to the nation-state—need to enter the mainstream of Indonesian economy, culture, and society.

The Basic Agrarian Law of 1960, itself a continuation of the colonial policy first spelled out in the Agrarian Act of 1870, does recognize customary law as the basis for national land law.[57] But this law is largely irrelevant to tracts classified as forest area under the provisions of the Basic Forestry Law. Few rural communities understand national laws and legal procedures. Most people have never heard of the Basic Agrarian Law[58] and—small wonder—even fewer have registered their customary rights according to its provisions.

A 1987 study in Irian Jaya province concluded that the process for official registration of *adat* tenurial rights in the central highlands was generally invoked at the instigation of land speculators from outside the community buying lands held under *adat* as insurance against subsequent claims by other *adat* claimants to the same parcel of land.[59] In addition, like the Basic Forestry Law, the Agrarian Law notes that community-based customary law "applies to the land, water and air *as long as it does not contradict* national and State interests" (emphasis added). Given this convenient legal rationale for overriding customary rights within a forest concession or protected area, the government routinely interprets the Basic Forestry Law as superseding the Agrarian Law in designated forest areas.

According to national law, tenurial rights to forest resources are determined by a classification scheme that recognizes community-based property rights, but the only tenurial right formally granted in any of the 30 million hectares of protected forests is to collect rattan. More generally, because traditional adat rights are usually recognized by national law only to the extent that they do not conflict with officially authorized uses of the forest, once the tide of state-sanctioned development reaches the region or resource in question, community-based rights are typically usurped. The Ministry of Forestry grants 20-year exploitation rights to private or state-chartered corporations, and indigenous peoples in particular often find themselves dispossessed. Outside entities are given "the right to exploit the forest in a designated forest area, through cutting of timber, regenerating and caring for the forest, and processing and marketing forest products…on the basis of conservation and sustainable production."[60]

Also impinging on community rights are the grants some Asian businessmen hold jointly with foreign firms. After being recommended by the provincial Governor,[61] applications and renewals are approved by the Ministry of Forestry. As of 1991, some 580 concessions averaged roughly 105,000 hectares each. Together, they cover about 60 million hectares, or 31 percent of the country's land.[62]

Another tool for expropriating traditional rights was introduced in 1990, when the Ministry of Forestry began offering Industrial Timber Plantation Rights to private or state firms and to officially recognized cooperatives. Recipients get a term of 35 years plus one growing cycle of the dominant species, and they can cultivate and harvest plantation timber on "unproductive" areas of permanent production forests. These concessionaires will, if current plans hold, develop some 4.4 million hectares of state forest lands by 1999.[63] This ardent pursuit of commercial forestry will further reduce national forest patrimony and further marginalize upwards of 60 million Indonesians who depend directly on forest resources.

Thailand

As in Indonesia, the military has long been the dominant political influence in Thailand. The Thai military, however, has not asserted direct control over day-to-day life and, for reasons not definitively understood, Thailand benefits from a more vibrant and developed economy than Indonesia.

Although the prospects for a new and more democratic government are promising, decades of narrow control have stymied efforts to identify and develop equitable laws and policies on community-based forest management. The Royal Thai Government, acting primarily through the Royal Forestry Department, still undervalues the conservation efforts of forest dwellers and many other rural resource users. Indeed, it has reclassified occupied areas within the *Pah Sa-nguan* as protection forests, plantation forests, national parks, and wildlife sanctuaries. People living in these areas are statutorily denied any recognition of their tenurial rights, making them legally vulnerable to eviction.

The most important legislation bearing on ownership of natural resources continues to be the Land Code of 1954. According to this law, anyone occupying a parcel of forest land as of November 30, 1954, was eligible to receive a claim certificate, referred to as *Nor Sor 1*, that could then be upgraded to one of three options:

- a certificate *(Nor Sor 2)* that authorizes temporary occupation of the land;
- a certificate of utilization *(Nor Sor 3)* that establishes that the person named in the document is actually occupying and cultivating the land; or
- a title deed *(Nor Sor 4* or *Chanode)* that acknowledges private, individual ownership or fee simple absolute. (Sections 1, 3, and 58)

According to Section 5 of the Land Code's promulgating act, claimants had 180 days to give notice of possession to a designated local official. Anyone who didn't do so was "deemed to have abandoned his right to possession," and the government could reallocate such "abandoned" land as it saw fit. As happened in the aftermath of the original land law, most provincial farmers knew nothing about the new law and so failed to give timely notice.

In 1961, a new military government responded to a growing deforestation crisis driven in many instances by migration, by decreeing that at least one half of Thailand's total land cover was to be permanently retained as public forest lands. Three years later, the National Forest Reserve Act provided the legal basis for setting aside these forest reserves. According to the 1964 Act, "within the national reserved forest, no person shall hold or possess the land, develop, clear, burn the forest, cut timber, collect forest produce or cause any damage" without authorization from the Director-General of the Royal Forestry Department. Violators risked imprisonment for up to five years and fines up to 50,000 *baht* (US$2,000).[64]

When the 1985 National Forestry Policy reduced the portion of the kingdom to be legally classified as forested to 40 percent, the Royal Forestry Department was authorized to classify slightly more than 20 percent of the *Pah Sa-nguan* as non-forest. The Agrarian Land Reform Office received legal jurisdiction over most reclassified areas and it was empowered to issue documentary titles to occupants or landless farmers.[65]

Although the 1985 policy technically met the proportionality requirements mandated by the National Forest Reserve Act, forest cover in many areas was greatly overstated and the policy had little local impact. To help achieve the 40 percent objective, the Royal Forestry Department devised a five-year resettlement program known as the *khor jor kor*, which allowed commercial reforesting of degraded forests, particularly in the northeast.[66] But an estimated 4.5 million people, many of them from hill tribes outside of the Thai mainstream, already occupied the targeted areas. Lacking any recognized rights to the lands that many had inhabited for generations and unfamiliar with national land laws, these tribal people were at the mercy of the modern nation-state. In 1991, the military began to evict them in accordance with the *khor jor kor* program, though public outcry and resistance resulted in a moratorium.[67] Abuses by senior Thai government officials who manipulated the Agrarian Land Reform Office in order to obtain documentary titles over areas previously classified as forest, meanwhile, erupted into a public scandal that culminated in the resignation of the prime minister and his entire cabinet in July 1995.

As of mid-year 1995, the government has not yet passed any community forestry law. An official draft of a proposed law called for the establishment of processes by which communities, except those in areas designated as conservation/protection forests, could gain some security of tenure over their local resources. Alternative legislation drafted by a coalition of non-governmental organizations provides for broader recognition of community-based rights. This widespread sentiment was captured in the 1992 Declaration of the Customary Rights of Local Communities by Thai NGOs which proclaimed that community-based rights "shall be recognized...as part of the law and national policy."[68]

Whatever legislation, if any, is ultimately enacted is likely to reflect the Thai Forestry Sector Master Plan's long-term goal that "rural people will have their rights restored to manage and use the forests." The Plan also calls for forest land reform that "will enable the villagers to acquire or to have legal control over the land they have [used] for many years."[69]

The Philippines

The Philippine government, through its Department of Environment and Natural Resources, has sole authority to allocate legal rights to use and manage public forest resources. Its policy accords fully with that of its colonial predecessors, who since the Maura Law was enacted in 1894, have insisted that all occupants of classified "public" forest lands are squatters, regardless of their length of occupancy.

The Philippine government claims ownership of more than 60 percent of the nation's total land area of 30 million hectares. As of 1994, nearly half of that total was either formally classified as "public" forest or is unclassified and legally presumed to be forested.[70]

Most of these areas are in the mountainous interiors of the nation's twelve largest islands, especially Luzon and Mindanao.

As in Thailand, the size of the public forest zone does not correspond to actual forest cover. The World Bank estimated in 1989 that only six million hectares contained "any significant tree cover," and that only one million hectares of "productive, old growth forest" existed.[71] The government maintains that about a fourth, i.e., 7.5 million hectares, of the nation's land mass is still forested.

Estimates of the number of people living within the public forest zone are equally controversial. Throughout the 1980s, official government estimates had hovered around one million. But a study conducted by the University of the Philippines at Los Baños' Center for Policy and Development Studies (1986) paints a dramatically different picture. Using official census statistics, it concluded that as of 1980 more than 14.4 million people resided in upland forest zones.[72] Assuming an annual population growth rate of 2.5 to 2.8 percent, an estimated 24 million people reside in upland forest zones as of 1995.[73]

Exactly how many hectares of forest are covered by community-based property rights is unknown. In 1988, the Department of Agrarian Reform pegged ancestral domains at about six million hectares.[74] Whatever their actual extent, these domains include much, if not most, of the nation's remaining forests.

Ancestral domains are defined in the Comprehensive Agrarian Reform Law of 1987 as including, but not limited to, "lands in the actual, continuous, and open possession and occupation of [an indigenous] community and its members." (Republic Act No. 6657, Section 9). The same section provides that "[i]n line with the principles of self-determination and autonomy, the systems of land ownership, land use, and the modes of settling; land disputes of all these communities must be recognized and respected." The 1987 Act also calls for the identification and delineation of ancestral domains but provided no mechanism or funding for this task.

The Philippines' system of land classification that was established early on by the U.S. colonial regime persists and remains the primary legal impediment to the recognition of ancestral domain rights within the public forest zone. Under the current law on land classification, classified "public" forest land cannot become privately owned. Instead, the government can recognize or grant private ownership rights only on "public agricultural" land.

The Forestry Bureau has long possessed the legal power to classify land as "agricultural"—a designation that basically allows for a private, individual title to be issued over the area. But the benefits of agricultural classification are enjoyed almost exclusively by those with the administrative and legal means to apply for private titles. For the nation's poor rural majority, the task is daunting if not impossible.

Further, the classification of public land as "agricultural" and its subsequent certification as "alienable and disposable" is not based on its overall biophysical characteristics. Instead, an arbitrary criterion established in 1975 proscribes such certification of any land with a slope of more than 18 percent.[75] The 18-percent slope rule is, in turn, predicated on the unscientific assumption that the Philippines' environmental stability depends on retaining approximately 45 to 50 percent of the nation's total land area for forest purposes.[76] The World Bank's 1988 study on Philippine natural resource management directly challenged this assumption about forest land use from both environmental and economic viewpoints.[77]

This same study concluded that "the main distinctions between alienable and disposable and forest land are legal and bureaucratic, not geographic."[78] In other words, the "classification methodology" was designed "to insure that sloping land (and any other land currently remote from markets), whatever its current land use practices, will be classified as unsuitable for agriculture and remain in the public domain."[79]

Disdain for the 18-percent slope rule is shared by people living in the public forest zone. As a result, one of President Ferdinand Marcos' last decrees was a 1985 directive to the Forestry Bureau allowing for the reclassification and certification of land in the provinces of Cebu and Benguet, regardless of the degree of slope.[80] Politically, Marcos hoped to shore up support in two densely populated provinces where large numbers of people occupied classified—but largely denuded—public forest areas. It was his failure in that election that ultimately brought about his downfall in February 1986.

The collapse of the Marcos regime, did not mean the end of the 18-percent slope rule and other decrees that usurp the community-based property rights of people living within the classified forest zone. Indeed, though various community forestry programs have emerged during the past two decades, people in the classified forest zone still live under legal threat of arbitrary eviction, as stated in the Forestry Code of 1975.

Sri Lanka

The limited data on the current extent and condition of Sri Lanka's forests are generally unreliable. But records do indicate that at the turn of the century, 70 percent of the country was forested and that by 1961 forest cover had shrunk to 44 percent.[81] The most recent survey of forest resources, conducted between 1982 and 1985, revealed that between 1956 and 1983, some 41,500 hectares of natural forests were disappearing each year primarily at the hands of smallholder farmers and fuelwood gatherers. Since then, forest loss is estimated to be between 30,000 and 58,000 hectares per year, leaving less than 24 percent of the nation still forested.[82]

Most of Sri Lanka's remaining forests are located in the agriculturally dominant dry zone that covers the northeastern three quarters of the country. Approximately 30 percent of the dry zone is forested, including 900,000 hectares in natural forest and over 100,000 hectares in plantations. Only about 8 percent of the wet zone (150,000 hectares) is still forested, down from 250,000 hectares in 1956. This small and shrinking wet-zone forest accounts for much of Sri Lanka's biodiversity: 94 percent of its endemic woody plants and 75 percent of its endemic animals.[83]

Since climate constrains forest growth in the dry zone, the Sri Lankan government wisely does not promote extractive commercial forestry there. Instead, it has set aside many natural forest areas for conservation purposes. As of 1985, some 359 forest reserves and proposed reserves encompassed 2.52 million hectares (37 percent) of the nation's land area. These reserves are under the legal jurisdiction of the Forest Department of the Ministry of Lands, Irrigation, and Mahaweli Development. The Department of Wildlife Conservation oversees an additional 747,528 hectares of nature reserves.[84]

Although the Sri Lankan government is conservation-minded, it also perpetuates colonial era attitudes by persistently and indiscriminately blaming local peoples for forest degradation. As in Southeast Asian countries, the chief scapegoat is swidden agriculture *(chena)*, which supports farmers on nearly 1.2 million hectares, or about 18 percent of the nation's land mass.[85]

The Sri Lankan government's official attitude toward *chena* is reflected in its 1991 report to the United Nations Conference on Environment and Development. While acknowledging that *chena* produces nearly 80 percent of the country's rainfed grains and vegetables and provides livelihood for about 250,000 families, it describes the practice as "disastrous" and asserts that "the decline in the area and the quality of the forests in the country [is] due mainly to shifting cultivation, illicit felling of trees, and encroachments."[86] As in other countries, Sri Lankan authorities rarely distinguish between long-term occupants and recent encroachers—between those who practice sustainable methods of shifting cultivation and those who mine the land. To halt the alleged forest vandals, the use and occupation of all forest and nature reserves is prohibited by statute. Without a permit, it is illegal to trespass in forest reserves, to clear lands, or to gather forest products. Upon conviction, violators face up to five years' imprisonment and substantial fines.[87] Implicitly acknowledging the impotence of this law, Emergency [Forest] Regulations of 1992 reiterated its provisions and upped the ante to a maximum of 10 years' imprisonment and a 500,000 rupee (US$10,200) fine.

India

Unlike in Sri Lanka, where post-independence deforestation resulted primarily from growing populations seeking to meet household needs, the deterioration of India's forest resources was accelerated by the government's active promotion of industrialization. In the two decades after World War II, the new nation tried to become an important player on the world stage. But while Indian lawmakers reformed colonial-era laws concerning agricultural and industrial property, they left the Indian Forest Act of 1927 essentially untouched. As a result, paper mills and plywood manufacturers became the primary beneficiaries of government forests. To promote a revenue-generating commercial forestry sector, the government also encouraged monoculture plantations, especially of eucalyptus and Caribbean pine.

During this period of state-sponsored national development, swelling and increasingly marginalized rural populations were left to meet their daily needs on steadily smaller and less productive forest areas. These deforestation pressures also contributed to—and were exacerbated by—the increasing encroachment of agriculture onto forest lands. These encroachments were periodically legalized (or "regularized") by state governments seeking political dividends.

Even though the colonial-era distinction between "rights" and "privileges" was never spelled out in the Forest Act of 1927, that distinction has survived in official documents and court decisions. The working assumption is that whatever access communities have to forest resources depends ultimately on government's good will, a point frequently hammered home in the state forest manuals. While the government has made it a point to "conced[e] liberal privileges...to communities which are reported to have enjoyed them," as the Gujarat Forest Manual puts it, the concession is a "matter of favour and not of right," and such favors "are subject to withdrawal at any time."[88]

This condescending tone is compounded by the Indian Forest Act's spelling out of elaborate—and often inappropriate—procedures for the demarcation of reserved forest lands and the settlement of "rights." Such approaches have proven cumbersome and are often alien to the settings where they have been put into play. They are also given to inconsistent application and minimal observation. Given the illiteracy rate and lack of national and state-level legal sophistication in many forest-dependent communities, current rules of notice, appeal, and settlement provide only the slimmest protection against the arbitrary extinction, diminution, or reallocation of rights.

For example, the Forest Act technically requires forestry officials to notify the affected population when an area is reserved, but the notification process is frequently poorly conducted, and the privileges conferred are rarely published or made widely known. As a result, according to a 1987 government survey, only a small percentage of a sample of tribal peoples had any inkling that they had rights to collect limited timber or to graze their animals on forest land. Others believed that they were forbidden to use the forest at all, while the vast majority had no idea what their rights were.[89] The criminalization of traditional practices is so widespread that many forest dwellers continue to assume that they are breaking the law whenever they enter the forest.

Official settlement procedures give forest officers wide discretion in monitoring practices within a forest area. Thus, the type of concession a community receives depends more upon its political strength or capacity to resist encroachment than upon the careful weighing of custom, local needs, or resource conditions. Also as in most tropical forest countries, low salaries make forest officials vulnerable to bribes and other forms of corruption.

Perhaps most alarming, giving privileges to local communities has not kept government from granting them to others as well, and outside interests commonly so deplete or monopolize the resources that the original privileges of the forest-dependent communities become meaningless. Nowhere is this more evident than in commercial logging concessions: on occasion the government has allowed contractors to clearcut large swaths of forest, leaving forest-dependent populations with pre-existing privileges only what they can glean.[90]

Since politicians and governments maintain that forest dwellers have no rights or privileges to be safeguarded, the forests are frequently used as demographic safety valves and low-cost arenas for development activities requiring large tracts of land. This approach often leads to the displacement of forest populations by large-scale development projects—such as the widely criticized Narmada River dam project in central India.[91] Typically, nobody makes much effort to assess the value of traditional practices or to find suitable alternatives, especially if the displaced populations are politically or socially marginalized.

In many parts of India, a long history of bureaucratic intervention has eroded customary rules and institutions. Deprived for decades of the authority to protect traditional areas, to punish, or to exclude outsiders, many forest communities have completely forgotten that any domains belong to them by usage.[92] In the resulting power vacuum, individuals vie for any extractible resources and come to think of themselves as poachers.

The ongoing destruction of India's forests in the nearly half century since independence has prompted several re-evaluations of the legal framework that has facilitated deforestation. Until recent interest in joint forest management emerged, most official statements on deforestation argued for *toughening* treatment of local populations and further reducing their access to forest resources. The National Forest Policy of 1952, for example, condemned the notion that "neighboring areas are entitled to a prior claim over a forest and its produce" and warned against meeting local needs at the expense of the nation. Numerous government reports in the 1970s—and even into the 1980s—insisted that tightening "concessions and privileges" granted to rural populations was essential to protecting the "national interest."

Nepal

Inspired largely by India's successful struggle for independence, popular uprisings against the Rana regime broke out in Nepal in the late 1940s, and open rebellion followed in November of 1950. After a brief but decisive battle, the Shah monarchy was able to reclaim full constitutional powers in 1951.

Over the next 10 years—a decade of considerable social unrest and political instability—Nepal experimented with various democratic reforms. Although promised earlier, parliamentary elections were finally held in 1957. But the quickfire pace of change was economically and culturally unsettling in a country just emerging from over a century of seclusion. At the height of the unrest in 1959, martial law was declared, and the new parliament was dissolved.

Before its dissolution, however, the Nepalese Parliament did pass the seminal Private Forest Nationalization Act of 1957, which abolished private ownership of forests. Pushed by donor countries and British forestry advisors, the Act sought to counteract growing demands for forest products, which—combined with ineffective management—had put heavy pressures on forest resources.

Good intentions notwithstanding, the Private Forest Nationalization Act is widely thought to have spurred the wholesale conversion of forests to farmland and a corresponding disregard for local forest protection.[93] Since the Act offered no compensation for soon-to-be deprived landowners, many purposely deforested so their holdings wouldn't be nationalized.[94] In addition, corrupt village elites bribed poorly-paid government surveyors to acquire rights to land that should have become nationalized forest. That said, much of Nepal is beyond the reach of Forest Department patrols, so the Act's overall effect is hard to gauge. Reports continue to surface of villagers who still have not even heard of the 35-year-old act.

The declaration of martial law and the establishment of the panchayat (council) system in 1959 brought a radical change in daily life. The *panchayat system*, a partyless but culturally rooted form of government, was comprised of a hierarchy of councils that extended from the village to the national level. In many ways, it represented a return to the traditional localized community governance so familiar throughout much of Nepal's history. In this tradition, popular participation has no place and power rests mostly with local elites.

The next several years saw a consolidation of central power accompanied by some disjointed legislative attempts to reform natural resource management policy. Strict usage-restriction laws reinforced the perception that government is an adversary in the management of local forest resources. Indicative of the government's hard-line attitude toward violators is Section 7 of the Forest Preservation (Special Arrangement) Act of 1967, which empowers district forest officers and guards to shoot anyone, below the kneecap, who imperils the life or health of forest officials, a provision which still exists.

In Sum

In keeping with their colonial legacies, South and Southeast Asian nations continue to adhere to Western legal doctrines and principles that don't *recognize*—let alone *value*—community-based property rights and management systems. According to these doctrines, nation-states legally own forests and private ownership cannot attach to classified forest land. Once the land is declassified, only express written grants from government can establish private ownership, a right that is limited to individuals, or other tenurial rights.

Management of much of the region's forests is now based on a mishmash of modern statutes, legal and business agreements with national or foreign entities (generally concessions for timber and mineral rights), and a wide variety of community-based tenurial arrangements. When these systems come into conflict, the government's inability or outright refusal to negotiate and enforce equitable outcomes undermine incentives for local-level sustainable management.

Government's presence in the forest neither encourages nor supports community-based conservation. Generally speaking, the more intrusive the interlopers the more the state supports their activities. As humanity's archetypal survivors, many forest-dependent communities, especially those made up of indigenous people, prefer retreat to assimilation—often the only prudent choice as powerful modern cultures advance. But where can they go? Only in myth does the forest go on forever.

IV.
COMMUNITY-BASED FOREST MANAGEMENT: EMERGING RESPONSES

Official reluctance to acknowledge the causes and magnitude of deforestation endures, but grave threats to forest resources and their local users is prompting change. Floods, landslides, and other well-publicized natural disasters have heightened both international and domestic awareness of deforestation's toll on the overall environment and human well-being. In some places, where flash floods brought on partly by deforestation have killed thousands of rural Asians in recent years, restrictions and bans on commercial logging have followed. In others, the reality of decreasing productivity and loss of environmental services has prompted the development of alternative forest management options.

Thailand's decision to impose a commercial logging ban comes as no surprise. The country's increasingly active media, combined with a growing spirit of democracy, allowed for a relatively uninhibited public expression of outrage after tragic floods. Threatened with widespread social unrest, the government not only met, they exceeded protestors' demands. As a newly industrialized country, it could afford to. With healthy industrial and tourist sectors (and largely depleted commercial forest reserves), the Thai government has come to rely less upon timber revenues.[c]

Other Asian countries are also trying to come to grips with the problems caused by deforestation. Each of the countries studied

---

[c] There have, however, been numerous reports of wholesale violations of the 1989 logging ban. In addition, many Thai suppliers have merely switched their logging operations across the border to Burma, Laos, and Cambodia. Although the commercial logging ban has had a significant effect on domestic Thai deforestation, Laos's 6 percent annual deforestation rate is the highest in the region and the world.

here has begun to address deforestation's symptoms, if not its causes. In all, equity and human rights concerns have come to play increasingly important roles. No longer merely the province of foreign-sponsored, do-gooder environmentalists, the sustainable management of forest resources by local stakeholders is emerging as a matter of justice, enlightened self-interest, and irrefutable need. In varying degrees, all six Asian states studied here show increasing public and governmental awareness of the costs of environmental degradation and its relation to equity and human rights, as well as a growing sense of the need for innovative and participatory approaches to forest management and conservation.[95] An integral component of these approaches must include appropriate incentives for forest dependent communities.[96]

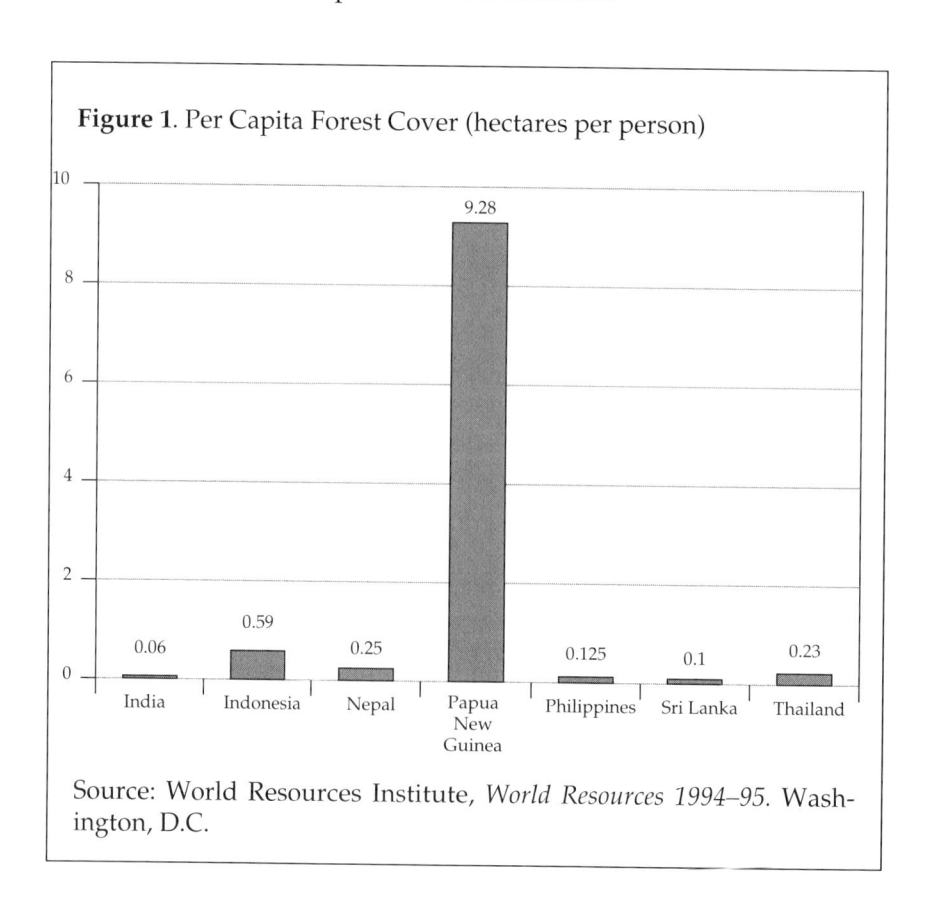

Figure 1. Per Capita Forest Cover (hectares per person)

Country	Hectares per person
India	0.06
Indonesia	0.59
Nepal	0.25
Papua New Guinea	9.28
Philippines	0.125
Sri Lanka	0.1
Thailand	0.23

Source: World Resources Institute, *World Resources 1994–95*. Washington, D.C.

India

India has addressed deforestation problems more constructively than any other nation in South and Southeast Asia, perhaps because with as many as 275 million people directly dependent upon a diminished forest base *(see Table 3)*, community-based forestry is an idea whose time could no longer be delayed. The current popularity of community-based forest management in India stems from popular agitation against the long-standing failures and inequities in forest department practices—unrest that the Forest Department could (or would) not suppress. Years of neglect and mismanagement, combined with acute resource shortages as population grew, highlighted the futility of stopgap remedies.

To date, India's joint-forest management initiatives appear to be working well. Over the past decade, forest cover decreased only 2 percent (from 19 to 17 percent of the total land area) while the national population increased by 23 percent.[97] During the first half of the 1970s, by contrast, annual deforestation and population increase were, coincidentally, both 2.31 percent.[98] The decreasing rate of deforestation demonstrates that forest losses can be mitigated and don't necessarily worsen as human population swells.

One hallmark of India's forest policy is continuity, particularly in the treatment of forest-dependent communities. Even today, many Indian officials believe that deforestation can only be stopped by bolstering the policing and exclusionary approach of the Indian Forest Act. A countervailing emerging approach, by contrast, emphasizes the need to involve local communities in forest planning and management. The rise of vigorous grassroots movements devoted to promoting social justice and sustainable development bolsters political support for the emerging approach. While the Chipko movement is the most famous internationally, many less well-known movements also promote—against tremendous odds—local control over forest resources as both an economic and environmental necessity.

Government policies have begun to show the marks of this new philosophy over the past decade. Most conspicuously, new forest management arrangements between state forest departments and local communities have been made, and an approach known as

"Joint Forest Management" grew out of scattered local-level experiments in the 1970s and 1980s. As of 1995, 15 state governments have adopted official joint forest-management "resolutions" (sometimes called "notifications") within the framework provided by a central government circular, "Involvement of Village Communities and Voluntary Agencies in Regeneration of Degraded Forests," issued in 1990, and others are now drafting such resolutions. *(See Chart 1.)* Reliable statistics on the extent of these programs are difficult to find, and it is too early to judge their sustainability.

Reports published in mid-1992 estimated that more than 9,000 village organizations were helping protect 1.5 million hectares of government forest land. In West Bengal alone, approximately 250,000 hectares of degraded forests have been rehabilitated by local communities under the auspices of joint forest management. Although these figures may include official projects that never got off the ground, overall they may be too low. Anecdotal evidence from the field is that community involvement in forest management is widespread and increasing. The official totals exclude many village organizations that have grown up spontaneously outside the official framework of joint forest management. Now that this form of management is officially sanctioned, reports of unofficial projects are surfacing. Indeed, village-level protection projects are spreading so rapidly in some areas that several state forest departments are having difficulty figuring out what is happening on the ground.

The official West Bengal initiative began in the Arabari district in 1972 when a divisional forest officer, A.K. Banerjee, worked with villagers to restore a 1,300 hectare sal (Shorea robusta) forest that had recently been commercially ravaged during a harvest. The villagers took responsibility for protecting the regenerating forest from illegal cutting, fires, overgrazing, and encroaching agriculture, and they were backed up by a forest protection committee that collaborated with the state forest department to set rules allowing participants to use the regenerating forest judiciously. In exchange for their protection and self-restraint, the villagers were granted access to a wide range of non-timber forest products and 25 percent of all revenues generated from the sale of harvested firewood and timber.

Emerging Responses

Chart 1. Comparative Aspects of Community Forestry Regulations in India

State	Product Rights	Responsibilities	Legal Personality	Tenure Rights
National	Community should share usufruct grasses, non-timber forest products, fuelwood, and timber.	No grazing, no agriculture, must promote stall feeding.	Villages or user groups within a village. No individual agreements.	No ownership or lease. Rights to use only. Renewable after 10 years.
Rajasthan	Rights to all non-timber forest products, 60 percent of net timber.	50 percent of net timber must be reinvested and must control grazing, fires, and illegal felling.	Group registered under the Society Registration Act.	Unspecified, maximum of 50 hectares per group.
Orissa	Rights to timber and non-timber products for subsistence, not for sale.	Must control grazing, fires and illegal felling.	Forest Protection Committee, registered with the Forest Office.	Unspecified.

Chart 1. (continued)

State	Product Rights	Responsibilities	Legal Personality	Tenure Rights
Gujurat	Rights to all non-timber forest products, 25 percent of government forest land, 80 percent of timber from other sources.	No grazing or agriculture, must regenerate degraded land.	Villages, *pinched*, informal groups, families.	No ownership or lease. Joint management agreement.
West Bengal	Rights to non-timber forest products, 25 percent of net timber.	Must first protect area for 5 years before taking rights to net timber and must protect forests.	Society registered with the Forest Office.	10-year rotation with the possibility of an extension.
Haryana	Rights to 25 percent of net timber, all non-timber forest products except fodder and fiber.	Must protect and manage the land, plan development and accounts, and form rules and regulations.	Society registered under the Society Registration Act.	Unspecified except on fiber, fodder, and bamboo.

Chart 1. (continued)

State	Product Rights	Responsibilities	Legal Personality	Tenure Rights
Bihar	Rights to dry leaves, branches, and grasses for subsistence, not for sale.	Must establish and enforce rules for forest protection, organize forest labor, distribute produce.	Village development committee; all members of 1 or more villages with tribal representation.	2 years, then a new committee is formed.
Andhra Pradesh	Rights to minor forest products, 25 percent of final harvest for local distribution, 33 percent of revenue earned through sale of remaining 75 percent.	Must ensure protection from encroachment, grazing, and fire; must assist the forest department to implement the forest management plan.	Registered by the Forest Department, no autonomous legal status. 1 male and 1 female member per household.	10-year management plan.

Chart 1. (continued)

State	Product Rights	Responsibilities	Legal Personality	Tenure Rights
Himachal Pradesh	Rights to usufruct (to be used according to existing agreements), 25 percent of net sale proceeds of final harvest to be invested in the village development fund.	Must assist forest department in planning, protection, afforestation, and general management.	Village Forest Development Committee, no autonomous legal status. 1 adult male and female per household.	Unspecified.
Jammu and Kashmir	Rights to all non-timber forest products, 25 percent of net revenue from final harvest.	Must assist in the prevention of trespassing, grazing, encroachment, and theft. With the Forest Department, must develop a procedure for sustainably collecting non-timber forest products.	Village Committees constituted by Forest Department, no autonomous legal status. 1 adult per household.	30 days after distribution and/or receipt of net income from sale of forest products from final felling unless determined earlier by mutual consent. 10-year rotation.

Chart 1. (continued)

State	Product Rights	Responsibilities	Legal Personality	Tenure Rights
Karnataka	Rights to dry leaves, lops, tops, grasses. Of timber and non-timber forest products, 50 percent goes to the government, 25 percent to the village development fund, and 25 percent to villagers.	Must assist the Forest Department in preventing encroachment, poaching, illicit cutting, fires, and unregulated grazing.	Village Forest Committee, registered under Karnataka Societies Act by Divisional Forest Officer. 1 representative per household.	5-year management plans.
Madhya Pradesh	Rights to all products derived from thinning and clearing. Some profit is derived from felling and selling nationalized forest products.	Must protect the area—prevent illegal cutting, encroachments, grazing, theft, and report to the Forest Department.	Forest Protection Committee, constituted by Forest Department, no autonomous legal status. 1 representative per household.	5-year management plans.

Chart 1. (continued)

State	Product Rights	Responsibilities	Legal Personality	Tenure Rights
Maharashtra	Rights to all minor forest products except cashew and tendu. Distribution of timber proceeds varies.	Must prevent encroachment, report crimes, help the Forest Department extract and store forest products. Must effectively protect the forest for at least 10 continuous years.	Registered by the Forest Land Cooperatives Societies or Forest Protection Committee. 1 representative per household.	10-year work plans.
Punjab	Rights to most non-timber forest products. All revenue from the community forests go to the community.	Must protect forest from fire, illicit felling, theft, and encroachment. Must assist range officer in planning and execution of afforestation and soil conservation schemes.	Forest Protection Committee. No independent legal status.	Unspecified.

Source: Adapted from Mark Poffenberger and Chhatrapati Singh, with assistance from Jonathan Lindsay, "Legal Framework for Joint Management in India," Sarin, *From Conflict to Collaboration: Local Institutions in Joint Forest Management,* p. 9.

In the crisis atmosphere that permeated thinking about Indian forests during the 1980s, successful experiments like that in Arabari and others in the states of Haryana and Orissa attracted considerable attention. Also important was the promulgation of the 1990 circular, which was spurred by the issuance of India's 1988 Forest Policy. Under this policy, the "first charge" on forest produce should be to meet the domestic requirements of tribes and others living in and around forests, indigenous inhabitants are to be enlisted in the afforestation of "wastelands," and "a massive people's movement" of women and men is to be created to achieve these aims and "to minimize pressure on existing forests."

Significantly, the 1988 forest policy is not law. As a statement of government intent, the forest policy defines no legal rights or duties. But its adoption did help create an atmosphere in which experiments in joint forest management could proliferate. It emboldened non-governmental organizations and community groups to be more creative in promoting community involvement and benefit-sharing in forest management. The 1990 circular likewise, is not a legislative enactment, but its clear support for participatory forest management marks the official inauguration of the Joint Forest Management Program.

References to Joint Forest Management as a single program, however, are misleading since it is actually a series of related programs adopted by state governments and implemented by their forest departments. The 1990 circular did not establish a single nationwide program; rather, it exhorted state forest departments to adopt policies and draft rules for implementing joint management. While leaving the task of drafting detailed rules to the individual states, the circular recognizes: 1) the need for participating communities and state forest departments, with as much help as possible from local non-governmental organizations, to develop and agree upon a management plan; 2) the right of participants to plant fruit trees in appropriate areas; 3) participants' entitlement to harvest minor forest products in accordance with conditions set by the State; and, 4) the right of participants to receive a portion of the profits generated when mature trees are harvested from the project area.

Conceptually, joint forest management represents a significant shift in India's forest policy in that it balances community and government interests while remaining sensitive to local ecological conditions, institutions, and forest dependence. Nevertheless, a closer look at the details and the execution of the various state joint forest management programs reveals that this conceptual shift is less dramatic than it might appear.

None of the state resolutions—nor the 1990 circular—alters the well-entrenched principle that access to and use of the forest depends ultimately on government's largesse. All of the state resolutions leave intact the basic property rights regime established by the Indian Forest Act. They authorize the delineation of specific forest tracts and the granting of certain conditional community rights to them, but the resolutions do not provide for the grant or lease of forest lands to local communities. In short, the state clearly remains the sole proprietor of the forests and does not recognize any community-based rights. Official participation by a community in joint forest management is contingent on the state forest department's decision that a particular area and a particular community make a good match for joint management.

All the state resolutions allude to local participation in planning, but none requires such participation. Thus, virtually all management decisions ultimately rest with the forest departments, including decisions of whether to accommodate community desires or to acknowledge community insights. If a participating community lacks significant decision-making powers, joint management becomes increasingly lopsided.

Other details in the design of joint forest management highlight the fragility of rights held by participating communities. Virtually all forest departments, for example, retain the unilateral right to pull out of an agreement if they decide that a community is not implementing the agreement satisfactorily. The lack of clear conditions and processes for terminating an agreement gives forest departments extra leverage to dictate or change the terms of a community's obligations. Once forest protection is under way, however, it would probably be impolitic to terminate an agreement for trivial reasons, given the current popularity of joint forest management, but this may change as co-management becomes more routine and the value of rehabilitated areas rises.

The treatment of timeframes in the state resolutions also fuels skepticism about the states' long-term commitment to community partnerships. In Jammu and Kashmir, for example, an agreement lasts until 30 days after the distribution of "net income from the sale of forest produce from final felling"—just a single growing cycle. In Madhya Pradesh, the management plan is limited to five years; no provisions are made to extend the plan if more time is needed to realize long-term benefits. Such short, fixed-term agreements could expire before final harvest!

Finally, the security of community rights in a particular area is weakened by uncertainty about the extent to which those rights are exclusive. While the Gujarat state resolution promises that the government shall "see that the selected forest area is free of claims from individuals other than members of village organizations," some of the other state resolutions are conspicuously silent on this point. In theory then, some states might legally grant rights in the same tract to outsiders.

In addition to issues relating to the security of community rights, are unresolved problems concerning the value of those rights. A joint forest management arrangement's long-term success will ultimately depend on whether the benefits a community receives (profits, increased food security, social stability, etc.) outweigh the costs of time, effort and materials. Obviously, joint management cannot guarantee a positive bottom line or alter basic ecological facts about the productivity of the land or the value of its resources. At issue here, rather, are problems with the way that joint forest management programs distribute costs and benefits—problems that can undermine or destroy a community's incentive to participate. Such problems are apparent in the benefit-sharing provisions of the original Arabari agreement in West Bengal. The agreement didn't specify whether the 25 percent of the harvest value that beneficiaries were to receive was to come from net or gross receipts. Since the state forest corporation handled harvesting and marketing, and the losses—aggravated by inefficiency and failure to sell at the best moment—were substantial, the community's total (post-expense) return amounted to only 6.25 percent. (Whether 25 percent of the proceeds is enough for the community is another troubling issue).

Other problematic issues concern the delineation of joint forest management areas, the resolution of disputes between communities, and the enforcement of community rules. Clear delineation of community forest areas is considered critical for successful management, and the process of setting boundaries has been controversial. In modern India, some communities have a clear sense of territorial identity with a particular forest, while in others, decades of bureaucratic intervention and internal migration have frayed the connection between people and forests. In any case, several communities may believe that they have legitimate claims to the same area and the granting of rights to one group may prompt others to feel unjustly excluded and resentful.

Ideally, joint forest management processes should involve communities and state forest departments in accommodation and negotiation. In some cases, dedicated forest officers and non-governmental organizations have worked hard to help neighboring communities reach understandings. But, if forest officers are made unilaterally responsible for delineation and assignment of areas, the state resolutions don't reinforce inter-community dialogue. If state forest departments and all affected communities don't communicate effectively, the boundaries of a joint-forest management area may bear little relation to traditional perceptions and local realities.

Another problem is the frequent lack of tangible government support for a community's right to exclude outsiders under a joint forest management agreement. Some state resolutions offer local forest-protection committees the right to "apprehend or assist (state) forest personnel in apprehension" of offenders. But how? Under the resolutions, communities have no formal mechanisms to exclude or otherwise punish such offenders. The state can prosecute and punish violators, but persuading forest departments and the police to exercise this responsibility is often difficult.

As communities reassert their control over specific domains, whether officially (under joint forest management) or informally, local forest users who are not part of a managing community can find themselves increasingly excluded. When protected areas regenerate, even more problems might emerge. The envy of nearby non-participating residents excluded from the project area is inevitable, particularly if more and more areas are declared off limits. Already, non-participants have looted protected forests, sometimes with the connivance of disenchanted community members, and there is now a growing need to enforce exclusionary rules. Failure to enforce can compound the original problem, and in extreme cases, a crisis of credibility develops and even community members start ignoring the rules they themselves framed.

In both Orissa and West Bengal, for example, new joint management agreements tend to cover large tracts. Non-participants are confined to smaller areas—one reason, some say, why so many forest-dependent communities feel it especially urgent to form protection committees. As former "open access" forests dwindle into parcels, nearby communities, afraid of being excluded altogether, rush to make their own territorial claims.

The 1990 circular doesn't provide much guidance here. It states that selected joint forest management sites should be free of "existing rights, privileges, [and] concessions." If a state forest department has already granted limited extraction rights to a community, however, should it then be allowed to grant additional extraction rights that overlap with the original project area to another community or legal entity? However fair and participatory in principle, this provision could easily create a (perhaps unviably) large pool of non-village participants.

Obviously, some problems with joint forest management are beyond the reach of local forest officials. A debate has emerged over the institutional forms that forest protection efforts should take. Most of the resolutions entrust protection to a voluntary, non-exclusive committee of interested inhabitants from the concerned village or villages. Yet, many joint forest management arrangements try to bypass established local village councils (statutory panchayats) in the belief that many or most members are not local forest users in the collaborating community and more generally, that the panchayat system has become corrupt, elitist, and non-responsive.

Why a new local institution such as a forest protection committee would be immune to the same compromising influences is unclear, but optimists note that these committees tend to be small socially and economically homogenous subgroups more interested in forest products than ruling elites generally are. Smaller, community groups (usually comprising 10–50 households) often mobilize more easily to establish local management systems. On the other hand, the danger that local elites may co-opt management structures to the detriment of poorer, more forest-dependent community members increases as the benefits of protection grow and become more evident. Nothing in the state resolutions prevents such a shift in power.

In addition, some observers fear that officious, bureaucratic state forest departments will try to standardize and formalize local forest management initiatives. A 1991 study of Orissa, where many examples of spontaneous protection are emerging, concluded that "any government intervention, unless well designed and implemented properly, may upset the fragile equilibrium within and among the villages."[99] However valid this concern, external disturbances may be desirable if the "fragile equilibrium" is maintained at the expense of equity, including the rights of women and/or those of sub-groups within the community.[100]

On balance, despite their promise and their early laudable results, joint forest management programs are products of the legal and policy traditions that have shaped Indian forestry for over a century. The details of their design and execution reveal state forest departments' continuing reluctance to give real enforceable rights to local communities while the half-hearted promotion of community participation in planning and the states' attempt to dictate bespeak a continuing emphasis on top-down management.

Valid though these criticisms may be, Joint Forest Management's broad endorsements of community participation in planning and benefit-sharing are significant advances over pre-existing policies in India. Enthusiasm about Joint Forest Management is sparking valuable local experiments (some of which burst the bounds of the Joint Forest Management framework itself) and the failure to completely reverse long-standing governmental control is by no means a categorical failure.

At this point, the legal clock can't be turned back in India. The social and economic dynamics at play clearly justify the search for new flexible arrangements that are sensitive to local variations. In its broad outlines, joint forest management offers an opportunity for India to combine the best of community intiatives and knowledge with the best that government support and supervision have to offer—but only if the now-fragile rights of forest-dependent communities are strengthened and made more secure.

Nepal

India's implementation of joint forest management programs is reflected in neighboring Nepal's recent commitment to revamp its community-forestry programs. Although the government continues to claim that it is "handing over" rights, local users' groups are being granted usufruct rights, not ownership, of forest resources. As in India, the government continues to own almost all forest resources. Even so, Nepal's "handing it over" program represents a serious attempt to break down the centralized system of forest management that has contributed to the deterioration of much of the country's fragile woodland resources.

Although precipitated by democracy's return in 1990, community forestry in Nepal had been a long time incubating.[101] The concept's roots trace back to long before the Shah Dynasty and Rana Regimes. However, its restitution began in 1967 with a World Bank-sponsored initiative that echoed popular desire to mitigate the effects of the Private Forest Nationalization Act of 1957, especially its disincentive to sustain forest resources. During the panchayat period that followed the 1957 Act, a series of legislative enactments laid the groundwork for a new approach to community foresty. The National Forestry Plan of 1976, in particular, along with its enabling laws enacted in 1978, explicitly recognized the importance and legitimacy of local communities' roles in managing forest resources.

Community forestry received more substantive recognition in the 1989 Master Plan for the Forestry Sector. This document enumerates the nation's five basic forest policy objectives and lays out strategies for realizing them through users' groups. Objective 3 clearly articulates the primacy of community forestry:

> The principles of the decentralization policy will be applied to the forestry sector by community forestry, which will have priority among other forest management strategies. Priority will be given to poorer communities, or to the poorer people in a community. If the availability of forest

land exceeds the needs of the local communities, the excess will be allocated for forest management in the following priority sequence: people living below the poverty line, small farmers, and forest-based industries....

The Master Plan also makes a commitment to gain the confidence of Nepalese women because they "actually make the daily management decisions." According to the plan's guidelines, "one third of the members of the users' committees should be women." All told, the Master Plan directs nearly half of all forestry development to the clearly interrelated community and private forestry sectors, and more specifically, to users' groups, which are designated as the principal vehicle of local action. Although the Eighth Development Plan (for 1992 through 1997) does not deal with community forestry practices at length, it specifically calls for constituting 5,000 users' groups during the five-year period and for transferring 252,000 hectares of community forest to them. To expedite the process, the Plan also pledges to remove bureaucratic and administrative obstacles that impede such a bottom-up approach. The new supportive policies are to be "more liberal, simple, and clear."

The Forest Act of 1993 builds upon the policy directives enumerated in both the Master Plan and the Eighth Development Plan. Over two years in the drafting, it has not yet been enacted. If passed, it would represent the culmination of many years of development and reform in the management and exploitation of the nation's forest resources. Along with its draft by-laws, the proposed Forest Act would outline a relatively straightforward approach for implementing a community forestry strategy.

As it currently reads, the Forest Act of 1993 legitimizes and promotes community-forestry users' groups in ways unparalleled in previous legislation. Under the Act, users' groups would be recognized as legally enforceable entities, and the Act provides for their formation, registration, and administration. Like the Master Plan, the Forest Act of 1993 favors community forestry by stipulating that "any part of the National Forest suitable to hand over to the Users' Group as Community Forest shall not be handed over as Leasehold Forest" (Section 30). The delay in enactment of the proposed Act reflects reluctance in the Department of Forests to empower users' groups and decentralize authority, and this reluctance constrains effective implementation of existing community forestry laws.

A key element of the Master Plan called for government officials—from the minister down to the district forest officers, rangers, and guards—to adopt a "new role as advisors and extensionists," but that charge too is still largely unfulfilled. In some instances, resistance to change is a matter of honest differences of opinion. But some motives are self-serving. In many cases, government officials fear, whether justifiably or not, that they may lose their jobs. In others, corrupt officials don't want to give up profiteering.

As in a number of other Asian and Pacific countries, many or most Nepalese government foresters do not support local peoples' rights to own or manage forest resources.[102] Traditional forestry training emphasizes the role of enforcer, and forestry legislation reinforces it. A case in point is the shoot-to-maim provision of the Forest Preservation Act of 1967 (retained in the Forest Act of 1993), which is profoundly antithetical to the aim of "handing over" the forests to resource-dependent users.

Whatever their motivations, these state foresters wield disproportionate authority over the entire "handing it over" process. A recent general survey concluded that 61 percent of Nepal's forests have the potential to be legally designated "Community Forests," an estimate that includes degraded, ecologically fragile, or generally unmanageable land that is of little interest to local communities. At the same time, all prospective users' groups must complete applications, formulate (and, if necessary, amend) operational plans, and file annual reports. For a predominantly illiterate rural population, such complex administrative procedures can be onerous. Because local forest officers are obligated to help applicants meet these procedural requirements, these officials have inordinate power over applications and renewals. Many of their decisions are based on extremely subjective criteria, and the right to appeal is limited. Thus, the potential for abuse and corruption is great, especially because forest officers are generally poorly paid and overburdened.

The bottom line is that until there is more to rely on than the goodwill and cooperation of the Forest Department, the prospects for community forestry initiatives in Nepal remain uncertain. That uncertainty was further clouded by parlimentary elections in November 1994 which saw the coalition government led by the Nepali Congress Party replaced by a coalition government led by the Nepal Communist Party. Although the Communist Party campaigned on the issue of increased land reform, how that promise will play out in terms of national policies and on-the-ground practices remains to be determined.

The Philippines

Official support for community forestry in the Philippines has been increasing steadily since the late 1970s. A driving force has been growing awareness of deforestation, and public concern over the issuance of large timber concessions that overlap with indigenous territories. After more than 5,000 people died in flash floods that swept down the denuded hillsides surrounding Ormoc City on the island of Leyte in 1991, public concern intensified and nearly spurred the Philippine Congress to ban commercial logging. That didn't happen, but since the demise of the Marcos regime in 1986, community forestry in the Philippines has become increasingly popular. Virtually no one publicly opposes it, and Philippine laws, policies, and programs in support of community forestry now rank among the most elaborate and enlightened in Asia. If anything, the Philippines suffers from a surfeit of laws and policies, many of which are more than superficially contradictory.

These progressive laws and policy frameworks have yet to be translated into effective programs. At fault is a lack of political will from the highest levels of civil authority on down. Real power in the Philippines remains in the hands of a few families who secured property rights decades ago from the hands of the Spanish and U.S. colonists and, more recently, used their privileged positions to gain forest concessions.

In theory, the more than 20 million people who live in classified forest zones have three major options for securing tenurial rights to forests and other local resources and for procuring financial and technical assistance. In fact, though, few know how to navigate the labyrinthine and often corrupt bureaucracy. Those who try must

Chart 2. Comparative Aspects of Community Forestry Projects in Five Countries

Nation or State	West Bengal, India	The Philippines		Thailand	Java, Indonesia	Nepal	
						Individual	Community
Legal personality	Community	Individual	Nonstock, nonprofit corporation	Individual Claim Certificate	Household[a]	Individual	Community
Direct use	Yes[b]	Yes	Yes[b]	Yes	Yes	Yes[b]	Yes[b]
Indirect economic gain	Land—no; trees, produce—yes	Land—no; produce—yes	Trees	Land—no, some trees; produce—yes	Land, trees—no; produce—yes		
Control	Yes[c]	Yes[b]	Yes[b]	Yes	Yes[b]		
Transfer	No	No	No	No	No	No	No
Residual rights	Yes	Yes	Yes	Yes	No	No	No
Participants	Anyone interested	Pre-1982 occupant	Pre-1982 occupant	Pre-1982 occupant	Forest-dependent people	Males	Males

Chart 2. (continued)

Nation or State	West Bengal, India	The Philippines		Thailand	Java, Indonesia	Nepal	
Duration	Open	25 years, renewable once	25 yrs, renewable once	5 years	2-year intervals	Indefinite	Indefinite
Size	Open	7 hectares (2–3 hectares average)	Open	24 hectares	Less than 1 hectare		
Cancelable by the government	Yes	Yes	Yes	Yes	Yes		
Year started	1989	1981	1984	1982	*Information missing?*	1983	1983

Notes:
[a] Signed on behalf of groups of households.
[b] With restrictions.
[c] Subject to federal approval.

start in the Department of Environment and Natural Resources through the Integrated Social Forestry Program,[103] the Forest Land Management Agreement,[104] or the Community Forestry Program.

The Integrated Social Forestry Program issues Certificates of Stewardship, mostly to individual forest farmers. Individual agreements authorize an individual to farm an average of 2.5 hectares of forest land over 25 years on a one-renew basis. As of year-end 1993, over 256 thousand individual stewardship agreements covered 586,000 hectares. Some 36 Community Forest Stewardship Agreements, covering 76,628 hectares, had also been issued. The community agreements have no proscribed size limits, and the largest single grant (14,094 hectares) directly benefits some 3,000 people.

The Community Forestry Management Agreements and the Forest Land Management Agreement emerged in 1987 from a nearly half-billion dollar initiative designed and funded by the Asian Development Bank and the Government of Japan. Community Forestry Management Agreements are typically awarded to a contractor who then hires individuals to plant trees in a designated area. Many contractors live outside areas designated for planting, though, and the agreements frequently overlook or violate local interests. As of 1991, the Department of Environment and Natural Resources reported that 1,315,815 hectares had been planted through Community Forestry Management Agreements, although the survival rate of the plantings has been dismally small.

The Community Forestry Management Agreements do not address the care and upkeep of planted seedlings. To address this egregious oversight, the Forest Land Management Agreement was developed to provide leases for the same 25-year period as the Integrated Social Forestry Program. Under this arrangement, communities contract with the Department of Environment and Natural Resources to manage an area and protect it from illegal loggers. In return, they are granted the right to harvest its timber.

All three types of grants can be cancelled by the Department of Environment and Natural Resources if the communities fail—in the opinion of the Department—to comply with the terms of the agreements. A new and fourth possibility for original, long-term occupants is to acquire Certificates of Ancestral Domain Claims.[105]

As the government cannot cancel the rights that these Certificates recognize, their popularity is growing among long-established forest communities. This non-revocability, however, helps to explain the resistance within the department to delineation of ancestral-domain perimeters.

The Department of Environment and Natural Resources created Certificates of Ancestral Domain Claims in response to growing pressure from grassroots activists and international donors to recognize the inherited rights of indigenous communities, most of whom live within classified forest zones. The legal basis for the Ceritificates is a 1909 United States Supreme Court decision written by Oliver Wendell Holmes that has never been overruled. *(See Box 5.)* In that case, the justices unanimously ruled that land occupied since time immemorial is presumed to never have been public land. The 1993 Department of Environment and Natural Resources Administrative Order No. 2 establishes a process for delineating ancestral-domain perimeters based on that decision, but as of mid-year 1995 government funding for delineation is still miniscule and except in a few areas implementation remains doubtful.

Through the National Integrated Protected Areas Act of 1991,[106] the Philippine Congress—under intense pressure from the World Bank—passed a policy to safeguard ancestral domains in biologically critical areas and to recognize the importance of community-based management of natural resources.[107] According to Section 13 of this Act, within designated protected areas "ancestral land and customary rights and interest arising shall be accorded due recognition." A later sentence—clearer and harder to ignore—states that the Department of Environment and Natural Resources "shall have no power to evict indigenous communities from their present occupancy nor resettle them to another area without their consent."

The National Integrated Protected Areas Act's implementing guidelines reaffirm this commitment. Chapter VII requires the delineation and demarcation of ancestral-domain rights in protected areas, and the participatory formulation and implementation of local management plans. Section 10 also mandates that "the zoning of a protected area and its buffer zones shall not restrict the rights of indigenous communities to pursue traditional and sustainable means of livelihood within their ancestral domain." But these laws and regulations are also not being implemented, and opposition to creating protected areas is mounting in many parts of the Philippines. Indeed, one effort to establish a protected area in Mindoro was stopped by local communities who feared being denied access to their traditional hunting and gathering grounds, or worse yet, being evicted.[108]

Another initiative with growing implications for community-based forestry provides for the conversion of traditional timber license agreements into Industrial Forest Management Agreements that authorize logging in residual forests only after degraded areas covered by the agreements have been replanted. According to Department Administrative Order No. 60 of 1993, prospective parties to these agreements must identify communities living within the target areas and give them notice of the application, and applicants must enter into mutually agreeable benefit-sharing agreements with local residents. Unfortunately, many timber concessions were converted to Industrial Forest Management Agreements before the Department of Environment and Natural Resources issued this order. So, many forest communities, especially in the large southern island of Mindanao, have once again been legally marginalized. In addition, many agreements made since 1993 have not been in compliance with the new order, a fact that reflects the tenacity of conventional foresters and their resistance to change.

Opposition to the Industrial Forest Management Program is mounting among forest communities and non-governmental organizations. A major rallying point is an agreement entered into with C. Alcantara and Sons, Inc. (ALSONS) that covers about 20,000 hectares in the province of Davao del Norte. This concession, and others like it, overlap with the ancestral domain of 19,000 Ata-Manobos. After many failed attempts to negotiate a moratorium on the implementation and expansion of the agreement, Ata-Manobo warriors attacked ALSON employees on October 20, 1994, reportedly leaving three dead and six others wounded.[109] Although this outbreak portends further clashes between commercial extractors and local communities, the Industrial Forest Management Program remains the preferred means within the Department of Environment and Natural Resources and the commercial forestry sector for managing Philippine forest resources.[110]

Thailand

The Thai government's recent laissez-faire policy on managing forest resources continues to invite intrusions into the *Pah Sa-nguan*. Along with abundant paddies, fields, and orchards that sustain millions of people, the *Pah Sa-nguan* now teems with industrial sites, vacation homes, golf courses, and district capitals.[111] Local unrest in Thailand over the allocation of rights to resources with forest reserves, national parks, and wildlife sanctuaries has also been considerable. In 1974, the government attempted to alleviate unrest generated by insecure property rights in forest areas by declaring amnesty for occupants of forest reserves who had illegally hunted, gathered, and farmed in them on condition that they curtail their activities.[112]

The following year, the Thai government approved a plan for a forest village program managed by the Royal Forest Department. The plan proved too ambitious and expensive, however, so the Department was ordered "to solve the problem by giving the people the minimum development needed for their well being."[113] The Royal Forest Department responded by instituting the National Forest Land Allotment Project. It allowed occupants of areas designated as commercial/production forests to lease up to 2.4 hectares of land for three years, but offered no tenurial provisions for community forests. People living in conservation/protection forests, meanwhile, were eligible to participate in the Allotment Project, the Department's original Forest Village Program, the Forest Industry Organization's Plantation Program, or the Agrarian Land Reform Office's titling project.[114] But, for all these programs, the gap between eligibility and participation is huge, although in 1994 there was a large increase in the number of rural farmers gaining provisional titles to agricultural areas adjacent to forests.

The primary goal of all current official community-forestry programs in Thailand has been to increase the number of planted trees. In the *taungya* system, "forest villages" are created in two ways. Villagers plant trees for payment, or they do so in exchange for the right to cultivate the spaces between saplings for a few years. In either case, the trees belong to the government. Through the community forestry or village woodlot program, the Royal Forest Department provides seedlings to plant on small tracts of public land (pastures or temple grounds).

In general, the Thai government has increasingly provided rhetorical support for the concept of community-based forest management; meanwhile, most forest-dependent communities are illegally occupying government-owned land. A proposed community forest law that has yet to be enacted might provide a means for recognizing or granting local rights. The revocation of the Royal Forest Department's requirement that seedlings be planted in blocks of 20,000 is another hopeful development and villagers may now plant a smaller number of seedlings along irrigation canals, by roads, or in their yards.[115] Some villages, however, want to plant trees on land in the *Pah Sa-nguan*, a practice local offices of the Royal Forest Department have accepted only informally since it continues to be officially barred.

The bottom line is that Thai foresters recognize two kinds of community forestry in the *Pah Sa-nguan*—one envisioned by outsiders (on woodlots, on *taungya* plantations, and through agroforestry initiatives) and one that is indigenous. Some foresters are trying to figure out ways to incorporate indigenous systems into programs structured by the Royal Forest Department. In its Chiang Mai regional office, for example, the Department is supporting a pilot program to recognize and legally authorize community-forest management systems not located within protected areas (including watersheds, national parks, and so forth). A flyer from the Chiang Mai Regional Royal Forest Department office lists one project that has been approved and six that are under consideration. Many forest farmers, however, are not interested in participating because of suspicions about future RFD regulations, limitations on the size of claim, etc. There is also a well-established tradition of avoiding interaction with the government as much as possible in order to avoid being compelled to observe unfavorable laws and regulations.

Given the mixed results of the scattered array of Thai forestry programs, the emerging consensus is that some type of innovative and meaningful community forestry program needs to be defined and implemented. The Thai Forestry Sector Master Plan calls for emphasis on forest-based rural development, and calls on forest communities and non-governmental organizations to catalyze and participate in rural development. The official first step, however, lies in the approval of a Community Forest Act that would classify and designate some occupied areas of the *Pah Sa-nguan* as community forests. This has yet to occur.

Although certain changes in Thai land laws would also help, some legal innovations are possible within current domestic and international laws. For example, rights of possession recognized in the Land Code are automatically and unilaterally extinguished whenever an occupied area becomes part of an officially designated forest reserve, wildlife sanctuary, national park, or more recently, critical watershed. This interpretation holds whether or not a designated area was occupied before or after 1954 when the Land Code allowed occupants to receive a *Nor Sor* certificate, but it contradicts the Constitution of the Kingdom of Thailand and other relevant laws. Indeed, Section 32 of the Constitution guarantees that "The peaceful habitation of every person in and for his [her] dwelling is protected." Even more important, Section 33, which protects "the rights of a person in property" *(sit ti khong book-kon nai subin),* does not limit the right to own private property to individuals.

The Civil and Commercial Code of Thailand (1925) identifies a distinct type of property right as a "possessory right." Section 1367 of the Code provides that "a person may acquire a possessory right by holding property with the intention of holding it for himself." Thai lawyers, citing Section 1307—"no prescription can be set up against the State with regard to any property which forms part of its public domain"—as support, generally hold that this provision does not apply. But to claim that Section 1307 renders Section 1367 meaningless misses the point since the Thai Constitution protects a person's property rights, and possessory rights are property rights. Many such possessory rights predate the 1978 Constitution, as well as the new Constitution, the 1925 Civil Code, and even King Chulalongkorn's proclamation of the mid-1890s. Many rights likewise predate their inclusion in areas designated as "forest reserves, national parks, wildlife sanctuaries, [and/or watersheds]."

By arbitrarily and unilaterally extinguishing long-standing possessory rights, even in the areas designated as conservation/

protection forests, the Royal Thai Government would appear to be violating its own constitutional standards. In particular, current procedures for designating areas as national parks and wildlife sanctuaries ignore the existence and legal efficacy of undocumented possessory rights.

This alternative perspective on possessory rights is reinforced by various provisions in the Thai Constitution that concern the rights and liberties of the Thai people.[116] International law provides additional support. *(See Box 6.)*

Sri Lanka

Despite a long history of local-level environmental concern and community management of water, forests, and other natural resources, Sri Lanka lags in promoting and institutionalizing community-based forest management. Although, according to Natural Resources of Sri Lanka: Conditions and Trends (1991), "public concern about deforestation and environmental degradation has never been higher in Sri Lanka,"[117] the national government has not formally experimented much with community management. The minimal level of official effort is no doubt due largely to the absence of the severe shortages of forest resources that have sparked and energized community-based advocates in India, the Philippines, and other countries.

More recently, however, the Sri Lankan government has begun to recognize the important positive role that some local forest users play in managing natural resources. The 1991 draft National Forest Policy acknowledged that "consultation with the community in forestry matters has been at a minimum or nonexistent in the past" and called for a change. (Section 11). The draft was vague, however, as to how this goal could be attained, asserting only that it could "be brought about through education and by using techniques evolved in the social sciences." Any meaningful community-based program will have to include some recognition of peoples' rights to use the land. Changes in existing Sri Lankan national laws would help, but current laws—as in Thailand—could allow important innovations. Article 28 of the Constitution, for example, provides that "it is the duty of every person in Sri Lanka to protect nature and [to] conserve its resources." In 1987, the 13th amendment delegated much power to the provinces, including jurisdiction for the protection of natural resources.[118] Once this delegation is more clearly defined, it could boost local participation in forest resource management.

Clearly, the authority to promote community-based forest management already exists. Even though the Forest Ordinance of 1885 authorizes the Minister of Lands, Irrigation, and Mahaweli Development to grant "permission to practice chena cultivation" in forest reserves (Section 9), it no longer issues such permits. Although this Ministry has never exercised its express statutory authority to "constitute any portion of forest [as] a forest village for the benefit of any village or group of village communities" and to "make regulations for the management of village forests," (Sections 12 and 15) that power exists. On public lands not set aside as forest reserves, the Land Settlement Ordinance allows settlement officers to set apart state property "for the purpose of a communal *chena* reserve for the use of the inhabitants of such village." (Section 5 (4) (c), Third Paragraph). Similarly, the Irrigation Ordinance of 1946 authorizes the official establishment and recognition of community-based resource management initiatives. (Parts III and IV.)

Until recently, the only government-sponsored social forestry initiative addressed fuelwood scarcity in local villages in five upcountry districts. Funded by the Asian Development Bank in 1982, this project failed largely because of its approach: local farmers were not involved in the project design or management—they were merely contracted to plant seedlings.[119] Compounding this was the fact that most of the trees planted were non-native pine and eucalyptus, not the more useful fruit and timber species that the farmers themselves requested on numerous occasions.[120] The planting of exotic species has also had adverse impacts on the wet zone forest areas. Despite the many protests by local farmers who have waatched their water table dry up where non-native pine, and to a lesser extent, eucalyptus, has been planted, the forest department continues to plant these exotic species—sometimes even in watershed areas.

The present ADB-funded project, begun in 1992, does allow farmers to plant whatever they want on a 25-year leasehold. However, as no contracts have yet been drafted with acceptable tenurial security, this project seems to be headed in the same direction as its predecessor.

In 1990, the Ministry of Lands, Irrigation and Maheweli Development commissioned the preparation of a national Forestry Master Plan. However, the World Bank-sponsored plan was prepared with minimal input from the public or from NGOs, and was criticized roundly when it inadvertently came to public attention during funding negotiations. As a result of both internal and external pressure, the government agreed to carry out an environmental impact assessment of the entire plan. A committee consisting of experts from the state, and both the private and NGO sectors reviewed the consultants' reports. The committee was instrumental in enacting a ten-year moratorium on all logging in wet zone forests pending further studies on the status of those forests. According to many, however, the most valuable result of the entire exercise was that it brought the Forest Department's activities into the public domain.

The 1990 draft Forestry Master Plan, meanwhile, was still being reviewed as of mid-year 1995. The importance of involving community-based organizations in the management and preservation of Sri Lanka's forests has been accepted as a concept. The revival of the Forestry Review Committtee by the Ministry of Lands, Irrigation, and Mahaweli Development was a major step in this process of acceptance. That recognition bore tangible fruit in 1994 when the Forest Department designated three areas in southern Sri Lanka as pilot projects for community-based forest management. However, a preliminary survey performed by Environmental Foundation Limited, a Sri Lankan NGO, revealed that these forest patches had become so degraded that neighboring communities no longer depended on them and were thus not likely to make much effort in their regeneration.

However, in areas where the forest remains still relatively undisturbed, buffer zone management with public participation is also being considered. In this context, homegardens tended from ancient times by Sri Lankan farmers abut many forest areas. In fact, recent surveys indicate much of the country's domestic timber needs are being met by these homegardens, which mix timber, fruit trees, vegetables, spices, and herbs.

Indonesia

Since the onset of Indonesia's commercial logging boom, millions of forest-dwelling and forest-dependent peoples on the Outer Islands have lost their traditional *adat* rights of access, ownership, and control. In a steady and sometimes complete process of erosion, the rights and livelihoods of local people have been subordinated to those of a relatively small number of commercial firms and state enterprises.

When government-backed development or conservation activities begin in areas governed under *adat* law and traditional resource management systems, local communities have few options under national law to defend their rights. One study of central Sumatra's lowland forests found that some traditional landowners did attempt to acquire land-title certificates to legitimize their adat claims under national law. But,

> for the large majority of local people, securing their rights through obtaining certificates is not a realistic option. They have but one possibility left: to force the traditional land tenure system to its bitter end, hoping that at least some kind of recognition will be given to them when the land is expropriated. Thus, their strategy is to clear as much land as possible within previously uncleared forest before somebody else does so. "We know we are destroying our forests, but it is a race and whoever does not join it will lose" is the fear expressed by villagers as they move to new forest areas.[121]

The crux of the problem is forest communities' inability to assert their adat rights in the face of government-sponsored concessions or programs. Consider the case of the P. T. You Lim Sari timber concession in northern Irian Jaya. In 1989, this concessionaire acknowledged a community's customary ownership rights and agreed to local leaders' demands for cash and in-kind compensation. But then the concessionaire began cutting in the village forests without paying the agreed-upon compensation. The villagers also complained that the logging operations were damaging rattan resources and destroying hunting areas that provide an important local source of subsistence.

Although some timber firms negotiate informal settlements with adat forest landowners, many establish their claim by fiat. In Central Sulawesi, for example, a logging firm claimed local farmlands as part of its concession area, destroyed crops to plant timber, and posted signs prohibiting tree felling and crop cultivation and threatening violators with 10-year prison sentences or fines of up to 100 million rupiah (US$50,000).[122]

Some of the disputes between *adat* landowners and development projects have turned violent. In Pulau Panggung in the Lampung province of Sumatra, local communities were informed in early 1988 that their crops (mostly coffee) and homes were illegally located on state forest lands slated for reforestation. They were given the choice of joining a resettlement program in another province or buying private land on their own outside of the designated forest area. Some residents volunteered for the resettlement program, but various restrictions on participation and allegations of extortion by local officials soon brought the registration process to a halt.

In 1986, Perum Perhutani, or the State Forest Corporation (SFC), which manages two million hectares, or approximately two-thirds of the government's classified forest land on the crowded island of Java, launched 13 pilot social forestry projects with support from the Ford Foundation. The projects required participating farmers to plant timber tree species (such as teak or pine) and allowed them to plant fruit trees and horticultural products in open spaces between the growing trees. Once the open spaces are shaded by tree canopies (which usually happened within one to four years, depending on the species planted) the participants were obliged to move to another site. This requirement and other problems has meant that overall, despite some improvements in forest cover and the lives of the beneficiaries, the project results have been disappointing.[123] In addition, despite the presence of tens of millions of forest-dependent people, there is still no official program or policy for establishing a community forestry program in the Outer Islands, although efforts are being made.[124]

In 1993, a Ministry of Forest decree authorized the harvest of forest produce, including timber, by traditional communities living within concession areas if they obtain permission from the industrial timber rights holder and authorization from the Minister of

Forests (Ministry of Forest Decree No. 251/Kpts - II/1993). This development is a potentially significant, albeit limited, step toward negotiating partnerships with forest communities and ensuring that they have incentives to promote sustainable forest management. As of 1995, however, even these limited rights had yet to be authorized anywhere.

Meanwhile, Indonesia's current legal forest-tenure system continues to work against the health of the nation's forests and the livelihoods of many local forest communities. Overriding constitutionally recognized traditional rights with nationally sanctioned rights and access rules undermines local incentives for long-term forest management and engenders social conflict. Compounding the problem, the sheer scale and, in some cases, remoteness of areas under timber concessions can overwhelm government's ability to collect reliable data, set boundaries, and police concession-holders.

A growing debate over forest tenure issues in Indonesia has revealed shortcomings in the system that non-governmental organizations, academics, and some international donors increasingly discuss and decry. Some Indonesian officials have also cautiously called for a re-evaluation of laws and policies and for experimentation with alternatives that would allow for more community participation and benefit-sharing. Still needed, however, are a strategy and a detailed set of substantive new directions for transforming laws and policies.

Lessons from Papua New Guinea

In contrast to the state-controlled paradigms that characterize the Asian countries studied is Papua New Guinea's (and other Pacific island nations') recognition that legal rights to natural resources are owned by communities, irrespective of documentation or Western-style acknowledgments. In Papua New Guinea, "under Melanesian tenure, resources are owned by groups but used by individuals (or, more precisely, households)."[125] These rights of ownership cover 90 to 97 percent of the island nation's terrestrial resources, including its forests.

The existence of state-recognized community-based rights provides forest-dependent peoples with a large degree of local-level

Map of Papua New Guinea

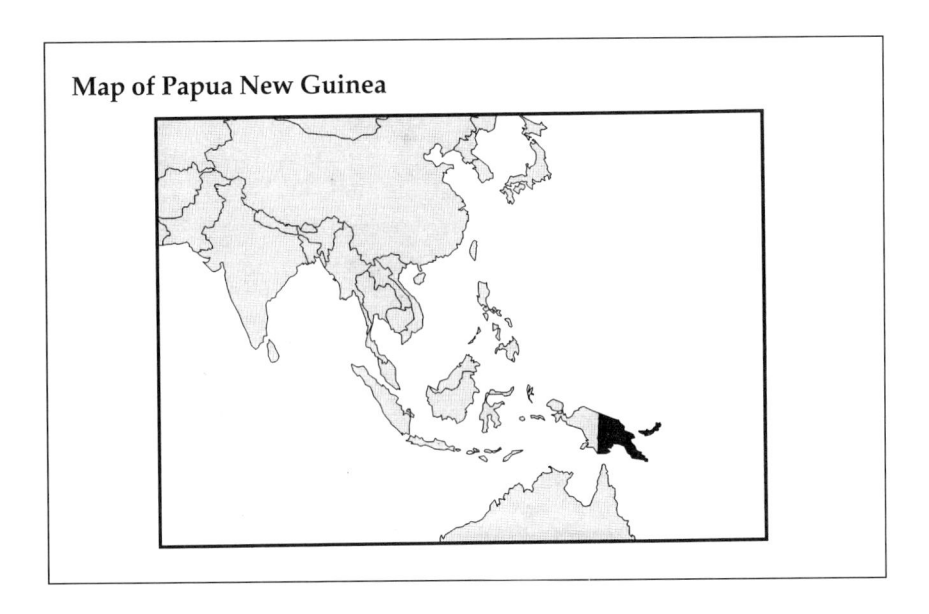

tenurial security, which this report considers to be a necessary but insufficient condition for sustainable forest management. Stories appear on a regular basis in the Port Moresby newspapers describing how a local clan has stopped a commercial logging enterprise because of misunderstanding and dissatisfaction over benefit-sharing arrangements. Frequent occurrences of this sort do not prove that tenurial security results in better local management, but it does highlight the importance of involving local people in resource management decisions.

Papua New Guinea has a rich legal history and much experience with efforts to forge a mutually beneficial relationship between government, local communities, and the private commercial sector. Many problems have arisen, but many lessons have also been learned. Indeed, Papua New Guinea can in some respects be considered a learning laboratory for identifying and establishing appropriate incentives that encourage partnerships and promote better resource management among all stakeholders.

Too rugged to be conquered and effectively colonized, the island of New Guinea was largely ignored by the first wave of European explorers. During 19th-century empire-building, however, the lands that now comprise Papua New Guinea were appropriated by the Dutch (who claimed the western half of the main island as a part its East Indian colony), the British (who claimed southeastern Papua), and the traditionally non-seafaring Germans (who claimed the northeastern portion of the island, which they called Kaiser Wilhelmland, and nearby islands to the north and east).

Put off by the island's inhospitable geography, the Europeans established only modest coastal toeholds. After Germany's defeat in World War I, Australia assumed England's role in Papua, adding to its domains Kaiser Wilhelmland, the Bismarck and Louisiade Archipelagos, and Bougainville. Occupied by the Japanese during World War II, when it was the scene of much fierce fighting, the eastern half of the island nation became a Trust Territory of the United Nations under Australian administration in 1948. Australia maintained only a loose watch over its territory, before granting full independence in 1975.

Papua New Guinea encompasses 46.3 million hectares, approximately 70 percent of which (34.2 million hectares) is covered by closed-canopy natural forests. But the country is so mountainous that less than half of its forests can presently be commercially exploited.[126] Estimates of the annual deforestation rate range from the World Resources Institute's 22,000 hectares (less than 0.1 percent) to the Papua New Guinea National Report's 290,000 hectares (about 0.6 percent).[127]

With slightly over four million inhabitants, 85 percent of whom live in rural areas, Papua New Guinea is spared the severe population pressures common in the Asian countries studied here. The national population density, for example, is 92 per 1,000 hectares, less than one tenth that of Indonesia, the least densely populated of the other countries in this study.[128]

Low population density means that the competition for land and other natural resources has yet to reach crisis proportions. To date, only in a few pockets in the central highlands and the Gazelle Peninsula of New Britain Island is population so dense that once-sustainable methods of swidden agriculture are no longer viable, and only in these areas is shifting agriculture the leading source of deforestation.

Since independence, threats to the sustainable use of Papua New Guinea's forests have multiplied. Although customary owners know they have recognized rights, they generally lack experience in the legal ways of the outside world, as well as the knowledge and training needed to exercise their rights in ways that promote material well-being and sustainable development.

As a result, traditionally sustainable forest-management practices are being undermined by modernization, especially the growing and often corrupting influence of the cash economy. To improve their own family's material welfare, some customary owners have sold their rights, especially to timber, in return for cash payments and other inadequate inducements.[129] Although many making these sales are clearly within their rights, all too frequently unscrupulous buyers take advantage of local ignorance and aspirations. By treating clan leaders to airplane junkets to Port Moresby and cash hand-outs that rarely reflect the value of the timber rights purchased, logging companies secure some concessions unethically, if not illegally. The cash received has long since disappeared in many forest communities, and many traditional areas are deforested and otherwise degraded.

Given Papua New Guinea's isolated and rugged terrain, commercial logging's belated arrival is not surprising. Nearby Indonesia, the Philippines, and Malaysia long provided a regional supply to meet international demand, and Papua New Guinea's relative inaccessibility and weak infrastructural development were compelling disincentives to large-scale commercial extraction. As late as 1952, production of saw and veneer logs was minimal.[130]

Over the past 30 years, however, commercial logging has become a driving factor in land-use change. Large-scale clear-felling began in the Gogol Valley of Madang Province in 1973. A year later, a new national forestry law authorized traditional landowners to sell their timber rights directly to private parties. Under this "Private Dealings Act," commercial loggers and local headmen were able to enter into Timber Rights Purchase Agreements without consulting either with the government or local co-owners. Few agreements made any reference to environmental safeguards, long-range planning, or sustainable development goals.

By 1979, with total timber output already nearly 20 times that of the early 1950s,[131] a revised and less stringent Forestry Act roughly halved the number of forest department personnel. By 1988, total output had nearly tripled again, with three-quarters of the harvest being exported, 90 percent of which went to Japan, Taiwan, and South Korea. Despite a 1989 ban on the export of raw logs from the ten most important commercial species, Papua New Guinea continues to be a major exporter of tropical raw logs. In 1991, timber exports, primarily to Japan and Korea were worth an estimated US$79 million—more than half what they had been in 1987.

In 1987, widespread and ongoing abuses and misuse of national forestry policies, combined with an alarming increase in raw log exports, prompted formation of a National Commission of Inquiry led by Thomas Barnett, an Australian jurist. The Commission's interim report, released in 1989, castigated the government for lax enforcement, widespread corruption, weak political will, and other failures, and summed up the consequences of the Private Dealings Act as follows: "In many cases, the timber industry has made life harder for the landowners at all levels. Not only do they have to face destruction of their environment, but they face the destruction of their society."[132]

The Barnett Report's indictments prompted various legislative and policy solutions. Concern about "high grading" (skimming off the highest quality trees) and a corresponding slump in the domestic milling sector led to the 1989 ban. Two years later, the National Forest Policy, drafted by the same Ministry of Forests so roundly criticized by the Barnett Report identified two main policy objectives: to ensure that forest resources were gathered sustainably, and used to promote the economic well-being and participation of all Papua New Guineans.

To implement the National Forest Policy, Parliament passed the Forestry Act of 1992. One of its more important provisions required the Ministry of Forests to reorganize itself into a professional Forest Authority overseen by an independent National Forest Board. But vested interests within the conventional forestry sector weakened the proposed Act by returning much of the decision-making power to the Minister of Forests.

The new Forestry Act also repealed the much-criticized Private Dealings Act and returned the country to an earlier mode of concession making, stating that "the rights of the customary owners of a forest resource shall be fully recognized and respected in all transactions affecting the resource." (Section 46) Customary owners, however, may enter into Forest Management Agreements only with the Papua New Guinea Forest Authority, which has "the exclusive right of cutting and removing timber from the area covered by the Agreement" and which alone can grant concessionaires rights to commercial loggers (Section 60).

Instead of protecting customary owners and their local environments, these provisions give the state increased power to usurp customary property rights in ways few customary owners can understand, much less influence. Recent trends in national law indicate that government is systematically circumscribing, and sometimes usurping, community-based resource rights. Usually invoked on behalf of such lofty purposes as the "public good," government appropriation of undocumented customary property rights harks back to the state-centric philosophies of former colonial regimes. All too often, the "public good" is defined in terms of profitability for domestic or foreign political and economic elites.[133] The Petroleum Act offers a blatant case in point by providing that "notwithstanding anything contained in any other law or in any grant, instrument of title or other document, all petroleum and helium at or below the surface of any land is, and shall be deemed at all times to have been, the property of the State." (Chapter No. 198, Section 5) Similarly, the Water Resources Act establishes that "the right to the use, flow, and control of water is vested in the State," although the claim is limited in that it "does not affect customary rights *to the use* of the water by the citizens *resident in the area* in which those rights are exercised."[134]

The Land Act authorizes the Minister for Lands to invoke (after two months' notice) "compulsory acquisition" of customary property rights "for a public purpose specified in the notice." (Chapter No. 185, Section 17) The Land Registration Act makes it impossible to transfer any rights or interests in land unless there is a certificate of title or registered document. (Chapter No. 191, Section 17(1))

The recently superseded Mining Act asserted flatly that "all gold and minerals in or on any land in the country are the property of the State." (Chapter 195, Section 7). This claim was broadened further in the Mining Act of 1992, which declares that "all minerals existing on, in, or below the surface of any land in Papua New

Guinea, including any water lying on any land in Papua New Guinea, are the property of the State," (Section 5(1)) though this same provision also says that "Nothing in Subsection (1) shall be construed as an additional acquisition of property in relation to Section 53 of the Constitution beyond that which prevailed under...all previous Acts."

Although it has yet to be judicially interpreted,[135] these provisions could potentially benefit customary rights holders provided Papua New Guinean courts define the constitutional terms "public purpose" and "reasonable justification" in the context of a democratic society and within the document's broader confines. Experiences in Asian nations suggest that the "public good" needs to be defined broadly to include the rights, claims, and aspirations of all citizens, and in particular, those most likely to be harmed by a proposed action.

The nation's most important legal foundation for community-based natural resource management, meanwhile, continues to be the 1975 National Constitution. Its fourth goal calls for Papua New Guinea's "natural resources and environment to be conserved and used for the collective benefit of us all, and to be replenished for the benefit of future generations." The language and intention of the fifth goal, "to achieve development primarily through the use of Papua New Guinean forms of social, political and economic organization," is equally direct. Putative tenurial safeguards also appear in Section 53, which protects Papua New Guineans against the taking or acquisition of customary property rights. These can be appropriated only if the property is required for a public purpose or to meet a need "that is reasonably justified in a democratic society that has a proper regard for the rights and dignity of mankind, that is so declared and so described, for the purposes of this section in an Organic Law or an Act of Parliament."

The state's slow usurpation of community-based rights may do more to undermine local incentives for sustainable forest management than the inappropriate exercise of local rights. More enlightened exercise of rights is preferable to undermining rights, and can best be promoted by providing local owners with useful information on resource management and extraction options, and on the environmental and financial implications of their decisions.

Despite the national government's ongoing usurpation of some local resource rights, however, the legal landscape in Papua New Guinea remains much more hospitable to local resource users than that in any of the Asian countries studied. The government and people have considerable experience with recognizing traditional community-based tenurial rights, identifying user groups, and resolving conflicts when claims and rights overlap. Yet, in Papua New Guinea, possession of state-recognized community-based property rights, by itself, isn't enough for sustainable resource management.

Efforts to formally recognize and officially document traditional community-based rights continue to be frustrated. Pressures on customary owners to sell their rights to natural resources are growing. During the past few years, three major studies have recommended the creation of a Landowner Awareness Project. A 1991 study, that was a by-product of the review of the country's Tropical Forestry Action Programme, noted that "awareness campaigns in Papua New Guinea have had an uneven track record," and cited two common reasons: project planners and designers have ignored basic and important communication principles, and models developed in other countries and indiscriminately applied in Papua New Guinea have largely failed.[136] The review offers two "guiding principles" for raising environmental awareness in Papua New Guinea. First, "effective communication cannot go in one direction only; it must flow back and forth in a dialogue process." Second, "effective communication cannot go very far without a set of shared assumptions and values...not only about communication itself, but also about the reasons and motivations for engaging in the communication process in the first place."[137]

In 1992, participants at the Conservation Needs Assessment requested by the Papua New Guinean government and funded by the United States Agency for International Development honed in on information management and distribution among customary owners. The main goal was to reach consensus on where biodiversity was greatest in the country and to set criteria and guidelines for promoting conservation in those places. This gathering of biologists, government officials, and representatives from non-governmental organizations and landowner groups—recommended that,

> An autonomous Natural Resource Options Network...be established to collect, create and disseminate information relevant to conservation and development. The [Network] should act in the public interest through: a) the development of broad-based awareness programmes on environment and development, and b) the provision of balanced and detailed information, especially to landowners' groups, on the available natural resource development options, their consequences and impacts, and the positive and negative development experiences of other landowner groups.[138]

The Natural Resource Options Network should be as decentralized as possible. For this reason, the Conference called for maximum sensitivity, accessibility, and responsiveness to local customary owners' information needs. Meanwhile, participants agreed that *before* government officials or commercial entrepreneurs encourage customary owners to exercise any property rights, local communities should be informed of the nature and extent of their rights, as well as their options.

V.
RECOGNIZING PRIVATE COMMUNITY-BASED RIGHTS

The need for local resource users to be better informed, of course, is not unique to Papua New Guinea. What is unique is that forest-dependent communities can at least expect to participate in resource-management decisions that will affect them. In this regard, Papua New Guinea and other Pacific Island nations are a global anomaly and a global paradigm. Throughout Asia and most of the developing world, forest-dependent people are typically seen as squatters on public (state-owned) land, even if they occupy indigenous territories.

Despite new rhetoric on the virtues of community-based resource management, and growth in the number of programs, projects, and, in some instances, even national laws and policies, few nation-states broadly recognize either community-based tenurial rights or forest-dependent peoples' contributions to conservation and sustainable management. Similarly, few countries seriously involve local communities in decisions over conservation and local resource management. Even though international legal protections are becoming more defined, their impact is still minimal. *(See Box 6.)*

From the viewpoint of forest-dependent communities in Asia, governments already have an overwhelming legal advantage. Under these circumstances, grants and other legal concessions from governments are probably the best that most communities can hope for in the near future. Until governments acknowledge the legitimacy of traditional community-based rights or permanently transfer rights management decisions, most forest-dependent communities have little option but to make the most of existing programs and lobby for improvements.

Box 6. Community-Based Forest Management Rights in International Law

During the initial phases of European colonization, community-based tenurial rights were recognized, at least in theory.[a] The foundation for this was laid by St. Thomas Aquinas two centuries before the colonization began. Aquinas concluded that temporal rule emanates from nature, whose dictates are universal, and he believed that natural law applied to Christians and non-Christians alike.[b] Under the principles of Roman law (on which the national law of the colonizing powers was based), however, ownership or dominion were rarely distinguished from sovereign or imperial rights.[c] Both Roman and Thomistic rights were thought to emanate from natural law.[d]

The 16th century Dominican theologian Francisco de Vitoria also argued that non-Europeans (that is, non-Christians) enjoyed certain rights. His lecture at the University of Salamanca (1539) "De Indis Prior et de Indis Posterior" built on Thomistic premises and concluded that American Indians had the same right to possess land as Christian Europeans.[e] According to Vitoria,

> The natives undoubtedly had true dominion in both public and private matters, just like the Christians, and neither their princes nor private persons could be despoiled of their property on the ground of not being true owners.[f]

Vitoria's theory held sway—at least theoretically in the Philippines and other Spanish colonies for more than three centuries: indigenous sovereignty and property rights could be expropriated only through conquest or voluntary cession.

By the 19th century, however, an ominous doctrine came to predominate that held land inhabited by people not "permanently united for political action" was deemed to be *territorium nullius* (empty territory).[g] This doctrine was used by colonial powers around the world to justify the wholesale usurpation of local rights. After independence, native political elites throughout South and Southeast Asia incorporated the doctrine into the legal frameworks of the newly independent nations, making it legally defensible to ignore undocumented community-based territorial rights and pretend that indigenous territories were unoccupied.

Box 6. (continued)

In 1975, the International Court of Justice rejected the doctrine of *territorium nullius* in the *Western Sahara Case*. This landmark case recognized the existence and legitimacy of indigenous peoples' rights in the former Spanish colony of Western Sahara. The International Court concluded that, at the time of its colonization in the mid-1880s, Western Sahara was inhabited by peoples who, while "nomadic, were socially and politically organized in tribes and under chiefs competent to represent them."[h] By recognizing the validity of government structures based on local, non-western, institutions and processes, the *Western Sahara Case* represented a fundamental change in international law. Of course, by 1975, many competent, traditional systems of governance had already been ignored and destroyed. Nonetheless, this decision laid a modern foundation for recognizing the legal efficacy of rights and institutions that do not draw their legitimacy from modern nation-states.[i]

The *Western Sahara* decision has become a rallying point for those advocating the recognition of indigenous peoples human rights in developing countries. The United Nations Covenant on Civil and Political Rights provides additional support for these advocates. One article of that document obligates signatories to ensure that the rights enumerated therein are "upheld without regard to color, language, social origin, property, or other status." Nations signing the Covenant must also provide "effective remedies" for any violation of these rights.[j]

The Covenant's Article 27, which mandates that ethnic, religious, and linguistic "minorities...shall not be denied the right, in community with the other members of their group, to enjoy their own culture," may have the most potential for promoting community-based forest management. Although the document does not specify rights to land and other natural resources, its language explicitly recognizes that

- smaller communities exist within larger nation-states, and
- each country has an affirmative duty to protect the rights of these communities as well as those of the individuals who compose them.

Box 6. (continued)

Another important international codification of the human rights of many people living in or dependent on forest areas is the International Labor Organization's 1989 Convention No. 169 Concerning Indigenous and Tribal Peoples. It provides that:

1. The rights of ownership and possession of the peoples concerned over the lands which they traditionally occupy shall be recognized. In addition, measures shall be taken in appropriate cases to safeguard the right of the peoples concerned to use lands not exclusively occupied by them, but to which they have traditionally had access for their subsistence and traditional activities. Particular attention shall be paid to the situation of nomadic peoples and shifting cultivators in this respect.
2. Governments shall take steps as necessary to identify the lands which the peoples concerned occupy, and to guarantee effective protection of the rights of ownership and possession.
3. Adequate procedures shall be established within the national legal system to resolve land claims by the peoples concerned.

The Convention adds that, "The rights of the peoples concerned to the natural resources pertaining to their lands shall be specially safeguarded. These rights include the rights of these peoples to participate in the use, management and conservation of these resources." International Labour Organization members are legally obligated by its founding charter to implement the Convention, but no country is in full compliance.

At the 1992 United Nations Conference on Environment and Development, the role of traditional and other local communities in managing forest resources was mentioned in several conference documents. Principle 22 of the Rio Declaration affirms the "vital role" of these communities "in environmental management and development," but it provides no guidance on how to ensure effective participation.

Article 8 (j) of the Convention on Biological Diversity requires parties to "respect, preserve, and maintain knowledge, innovations and practices of indigenous and local communities embodying traditional lifestyles relevant for the conservation and sustainable use of biological diversity." This language appears to provide a framework for interna-

Box 6. (continued)

tional legal protection for certain types of local community forestry management systems. However, this section is made "subject to legislation," a qualification which potentially vitiates its effectiveness.

Chapter 32 of *Agenda 21*, guidelines for realizing sustainable development at the international, national, and local levels, is directed at the interests of "farmers" which the document identifies as "all rural people who derive their livelihood from activities such as farming, fishing, and forest harvesting." It calls upon national governments to give effective land tenure to these groups and notes that the absence of legislation to indicate land rights "has been an obstacle in taking action against land degradation in many farming communities in developing countries." *Agenda 21* is not a legally binding document. However, the above pronouncements are bold and far-reaching in light of the emotive political overtones connected with resource use and land redistribution in many developing countries.

In 1993, during the World Conference on Human Rights, the Vienna Declaration and Programme of Action was promulgated. Paragraph 20 links sustainable development with equity and thereby implicitly identifies what is lacking in most international instruments dealing with forest management.

The recently negotiated Desertification Convention recognizes the rights and interests of community-based resource users as well as the participation of these groups as essential for sustainable natural resource management and development. Article 10 of this Convention calls for national action programs that delineate the respective roles of governments, local communities and land users, and which "provide for effective participation at the local, national, and regional levels" in policy planning and implementation. These sections are also "subject to national legislation" which could weaken implementation. However, the Convention evidences an emerging acceptance in international law of the need to involve local communities in the implementation of resource rehabilitation and management treaties.

Notes
  a. Mark F. Lindley, *The Acquisition and Government of Backward Territory in International Law Being a Treatise on the Law and Practice*

Box 6. (continued)

   Relating to Colonial Expansion (London: Longmans, Green, 1926), 338–353.
b. *Summa Theologica*, II-II, Question 10, 10th Article.
c. Lindley, *see note a*, 337.
d. Ibid, 10.
e. English translations can be found in Scott 1934, Appendixes A and B.
f. Francisco de Vitoria Address in Commemoration of His Lectures (Washington, D.C.: Catholic University of America, 1539) Section I, Twenty-fourth premise.
g. Lindley, *see note 80.*
h. Paragraph 81. Portions reprinted in Myers McDougal and W. Michael Reisman, eds., *International Law in Contemporary Perspective* (Mineola, NY: Foundation Press, 1981) 639–658. *See also* W. Michael Reisman. "Protecting Indigenous Rights in International Adjudication," *American Journal of International Law*, Vol. 89, pp. 341–62 (1995).
i. The decision left unresolved the standards to be used in determining whether an indigenous group is "socially and politically organized" and possesses "competent" leaders and representatives.
j. Other relevant sections include Article 1.1 which recognizes that "[a]ll peoples have the rights to self-determination." This encompasses the right to "freely determine their political status and freely pursue their economic, social and cultural development." Article 1.2 is more explicit: it provides that "in no case may a people be deprived of its own means of subsistence." Massive, state-sanctioned displacement of peasants and tribal peoples would, by definition, be a violation of this article. Article 16 adds that "everyone shall have the right to recognition everywhere as a person before the law." Article 17 proscribes "arbitrary…interference with…privacy, family [and] home." The rights of "peaceful assembly" and freedom of association" are recognized in Articles 21 and 22. The right to participate in public affairs is acknowledged in Article 25.

Prepared with assistance from Gregory Maggio.

Community-based property rights and management, of course, often exists even where their legal status is unsupported by government. In the Asian countries studied here, government mandates to manage and control forest resources far exceed institutional and logistical capacity. As a result, tens of millions of people, many of whom have lived on their land for generations, still manage and occupy forest areas now supposedly owned and managed by their governments. A lesser but still significant number manage these resources sustainably.

Laws and policies that ignore existing rights and management systems, and promote the tenurial insecurity of forest-dependent communities, ignore the obvious: rational human beings, regardless of their status or education level, are unlikely to invest labor and resources in sustainable management without some assurance that they or their heirs will reap the benefits. Empirical evidence from the countries studied and elsewhere shows that farmers and peasants are skeptical of government programs that provide them with only limited tenure in local forests and other natural resources.[139]

Where local communities practice sustainable management, or at least aspire to, and want governmental recognition of their community-based property rights, the basic components of successful state-community management initiatives are largely in place. If a mutually beneficial and supportive agreement can be reached, the odds that the resource base will be protected by local stewardship increase. An agreement can provide a cost-saving alternative to state management approaches that are by and large failing. Yet, except perhaps in India and maybe Nepal and the Philippines, this community-based scenario is unlikely to be widespread any time soon in South and Southeast Asia.

As of 1995, bureaucracies legally in charge of forest resources and their primary beneficiaries, i.e., commercial concessionaires, are tenaciously clinging to their privileged positions. As such, most emerging community-forestry programs, at best, grant only limited local rights. Even in India's relatively progressive joint forest management programs, the colonial-era perception that all local level forest use is a state-granted privilege survives. Nepal's recent—but still unenacted—community-forestry legislation and the Philippines' regulations on delineating ancestral-domain claims, for example, rest on the historically inspired official view that forest communities—including indigenous groups—do not own land or forest resources, but rather illegally reside on and use government-owned resources.

Perhaps even more disturbing, government-granted tenurial rights lack durability. What governments give, governments can take away, and most communities don't have the means to ensure that their limited state-granted rights will not be cancelled on an official whim.

Official policies that grant rights to certain forest resources but retain state ownership of the land also perpetuate various legal conundrums: do the tree roots belong to the community or the state? And who owns fallen branches or organic material when it composts into the ground? Such questions get at the practical core of local users' rights over natural resources. If governments believe that local communities must have a role if forests are to be sustainably managed, then the tenurial package should be expanded and strengthened accordingly.

State Recognition Versus State Grants

Although governments may view land and other forest resources as public, forest-dependent communities often consider them private. Whether a tenurial right is considered private or public depends largely on the viewpoint of the stakeholder. In the Asian countries studied here, governments consider large tracts of forests (including clearings designated as forests), along with the water and mineral resources on them "public." Communities, by contrast, dependent on or living near these areas often consider the same resources "private." And most established forest-dependent communities believe that, whether they own local resources or not, those resources belong to them. In this regard, the differences between what national laws say and what actually happens can be profound.

The tenurial security required for effective community-based forest management does not require that there be state-sanctioned and documented statutory rights. More important is governments' fulfillment of their responsibility to help forest-dependent communities defend and benefit from sustainably managed forest resources, whether public or private. Furthermore, property rights are not—nor should they necessarily be—contingent on state grants or formal documentation. Community-based property rights *by definition* emanate from communities. *(See Box 7.)* As such, in many instances it is more appropriate for governments to recognize existing community-based rights than to grant rights based on state claims of ownership.

Box 7. Preserving Community Rights in Arunachal Pradesh

The application of colonial land and forestry laws in India helped undermine community systems of resource management, and the colonizers were aware of this effect. Over the decades, numerous observers noted with growing concern the social and economic disruptions occurring in areas of India that were home to tribal peoples. Exploitation of tribal peoples by outsiders, and the associated problems of debt and land loss, were frequently deplored in the records of the more perceptive colonial officials, as well as reported in the works of noted ethnologists, such as Verrier Elwin.

In the remote forested areas of Northeast India a distinctly different approach was adopted. This mountainous area of approximately 81,500 square kilometers now comprises the state of Arunachal Pradesh, formerly known as the North East Frontier Agency (NEFA). It borders Tibet, Myanmar, Bhutan, and the state of Assam and houses some of India's richest forests. It is home to tribes who speak Tibeto-Burman languages, though extreme isolation means that many of the languages cannot be understood by other tribes. The population as of 1981 was only 628,050, resulting in a density much less than the national average. Of a total cultivated area of 133,435 hectares, 101,329 or 76 percent are subject to shifting cultivation.[a]

As early as 1873, the British government made efforts to keep outsiders out of this area. It established the so-called "Inner Line" along the bordering foothills. People from the lowlands were not allowed to cross this line without a permit, and the acquisition of legal rights to land by outsiders was forbidden. The formal colonial administration was slow to penetrate the region, and in many areas the

Box 7 (continued)

government simply had no presence at all. For the most part, the colonial policy was to allow local communities to enforce their own rules and traditions.[b]

After independence in 1947, this general policy was continued. The Inner Line regulations remained in effect, and the region was accorded special status under the Sixth Schedule of the Indian Constitution, thus giving a degree of community autonomy unparalleled in other parts of India. With respect to forests, one official circular issued near the time of independence highlighted the difference between the philosophy applied to NEFA and to the rest of the country: forest policy in the region is to be conditioned, the document declares, "by the direct interests of the people and not by our desire to increase revenue by launching upon a policy of exploitation of forests identical with that in other parts of the country."[c]

The overall emphasis on customary rules regarding forests and land tenure was encapsulated in the Jhum Land Regulations of 1947–48. Under these Regulations, communities are given absolute rights over their jhum-land—that is, "all lands which any member or members of a village or a community have a customary right to cultivate by means of shifting cultivation or to utilize by clearing jungle or grazing livestock, provided that such village or community is in a permanent location." "Permanence" here does not mean a fixed location; instead, it means the permanent location of a community within a particular area, even if the settlement migrates from place to place within that area.

The Regulations established several categories of forests. As in other parts of India, "Forest Reserves" are under the direct control of the state forest department. So far, this category applies to a relatively small amount of land. A second and much larger category consists of forests within the traditionally recognized boundaries of villages. These come under the control of existing tribal councils. In such forests, local customs and traditions take precedence over any outside regulation by the state. The amount of land in this category is a little uncertain. According to one estimate, "about 73.56 percent of the total forest area is marked as unclassed state forest land where customary laws prevail and the state cannot intervene without prior consultation with village authorities."[d]

Box 7 (continued)

These regulations contrast remarkably with the letter and spirit of the Indian Forest Act of 1927 (and its associated state-level laws) that prevails throughout the rest of India. Not only are traditional rights to land explicitly recognized, but shifting cultivation—so excoriated and repressed elsewhere on the subcontinent—is accepted as a given. In most of India, as in many other countries, much of the land not permanently cultivated is treated as not belonging to any one, and thus under the control of the state. By contrast, local perceptions of land "belonging" to a community, even when not permanently cultivated, are given far greater legal recognition in Arunachal Pradesh. In addition, the rights of village councils to the revenue derived from exploiting "their" forests are clearly set forth.

Despite its comparatively favorable status, the situation in Arunachal Pradesh has deteriorated in recent years. Increased contact with the outside world and improved communications and transportation have weakened community institutions. More important, commercial pressure on Arunachal's forests has increased drastically as India's overall forest stocks have declined. Local institutions often lack the sophistication or the strength to deal effectively with outside entrepreneurs, and the lure of wealth has prompted many communities to sell village forests. Reportedly, villages are scrambling to assert authority over unallocated forests so they can take advantage of the current market.[e]

Notes
a. UNESCO/UNEP, *Swidden Cultivation in Asia, Volume Three* (Bangkok: UNESCO Office for Education in Asia and the Pacific, 1985), 19.
b. Verrier Elwin, *A Philosophy for NEFA* (Shillong, 1964), 66.
c. Ibid, 67–68.
d. "Arunachal Pradesh's Fading Forests," *Down to Earth*, May 31, 1992, vol. 1, no. 1.
e. Ibid.

Source: Jonathan Lindsay

In a few locales in the Philippines, the government is preparing to delineate the boundaries of territories occupied by some indigenous peoples who are amenable to the idea and to issue a tentative form of recognition, Certificates of Ancestral Domain Claims to those communities. If it comes, this recognition may promote a partnership and help communities maintain and adapt community-based rights within territories that they deem private. Nevertheless, the Philippine government will likely still consider the land and forests to be public.

Private Community-Based Rights

This report concludes that government-sponsored community forestry programs based on public grants that can be cancelled don't provide adequate incentives for sustainable community-based forest resource management. Wherever local people are striving to protect and sustainably manage forests the best way to establish and secure these incentives is to get appropriate government agencies and officials to recognize existing community-based rights and to consider them as being private. This way, holders of such rights would have the same protection as owners of other private property rights. Governments can express this commitment through national laws and policies prior to any on-the-ground activities, although the spatial perimeters of community-based management systems should be delineated as soon as possible.

Besides providing greater assurance than existing programs that local people will profit from investments of their time and labor, recognition of private community-based rights would contribute to goodwill between local communities and governments. It would also provide communities with state-sanctioned authority to prevent migration into their forest areas. Technical assistance to develop organizational capacity and support sustainable management would, along with expanded credit programs, complement such a move.

Recognition of private community-based rights can help modify and better balance the relationships between government and local communities. In Papua New Guinea, a fairly secure—albeit threatened—balance has been established. As private-rights holders, communities can legally oblige their governments to consult them and win their cooperation before starting conservation or development initiatives and also to give notice and compensation before expropriating rights for public purposes.[d]

No property rights are absolute. All public and private property rights within national boundaries are regulated to some degree. Yet, actual human practices eventually define the limits and directions of all tenure regimes—from fee simple to leasehold to restrictive usufruct—more fully than formal legal frameworks do. The operative realities of land use and ownership are far more complicated and contradictory than the state-centric, top-down principles embedded in most national legal structures.

Whether public or private, natural resource tenure encompasses a bundle of rights. Terms such as "ownership" and "leasehold"—often used by outsiders to describe community-based tenurial rights—imply a Western concept of ownership generally at odds with the principles and practices of community-based tenure. Tenure systems are invariably complex and specify under what circumstances and to what extent certain resources are available to individuals and communities—to inhabit, to harvest, to inherit, to hunt and gather on, and so forth.

Governments that recognize or grant community tenurial rights, or persist in promoting the status quo, meanwhile, should all still work to ensure that sustainable forestry objectives are being met, and should intervene when they are not. Zoning laws exemplify this traditional governmental prerogative. Recognizing private community-based rights might also help governments raise money. One option would be to levy taxes, though tax assessments should never be applied indiscriminately to all areas encompassed by community-based forest management systems. Property taxes

---

[d] If a particular community understands and is comfortable with a government's failure to recognize its community-based tenurial rights, the community's view should be respected. Some communities fear that efforts to gain recognition of their rights will draw unwanted attention and generate more problems than are addressed. Such decisions likewise make sense when a community has the capacity to resist territorial encroachment and when the likelihood of gaining recognition is low.

might be justifiable on arable land, but on sustainably managed forests they are not since the community is essentially providing a service worth as much—if not more—than a tax payment. On the other hand, taxes on the sale of forest products, including timber, might be appropriate.

Private community-based tenurial rights should not be promoted on the naive assumption that communities always make the right ecological decisions. Indeed, usufruct agreements such as certificates, leases, or other restrictive tenurial instruments can be workable in some circumstances, but these instruments don't appear to achieve long-term sustainable objectives effectively because few leaseholders make the costly investments required to realize long-term gains. According to the economist, Theodore Panayotou (1989):

> Usufruct certificates or land titles for a specified period of time after which property rights expire do not provide the right incentives for investment and conservation. Only investments that can yield sufficient benefits within the given time frame of the rights will be undertaken, and exploitative behavior will ensue as the expiration date approaches unless there is a high probability that the property right will be renewed or extended.[140]

As is evident in Papua New Guinea, recognizing private community-based rights also does not mean that government or commercial interests won't be involved in resource management. Rather, the commitment will make local communities that are helping to protect and sustainably develop forest resources more likely to participate substantively in, and contribute to, future resource-management decisions. Simply stated, private community-based rights tend to provide more durable incentives and be less susceptible to usurpation by outside interests than are public forest leases.

One caveat deserves mention here. Policies recognizing (or granting) community rights might rest on inequitable community-based patterns of allocation and power relationships. In India, for example, some joint forest management agreements further marginalize women from the economic mainstream. Clearly, commitment to gender equity should be structured into community-based forestry policies and programs, as should concern for children, the elderly, and any other traditionally marginalized groups within a community. *(See Box 8, Gender Considerations.)* More generally, policy-makers and planners need to be sensitive to the blinding power of the status quo.

Box 8. Gender and Community Forest Management

Throughout the developing world, women have traditionally been responsible for gathering non-timber forest products (especially fuelwood) for family use and for sale—while men engage in agriculture and timber production. Numerous studies show that in many parts of Asia rural women are very knowledgeable about forest resources and management and work hard to protect and reforest land. However, both national laws and local institutions largely neglect their needs.

Mirroring their state-sanctioned counterparts, most community-based forest management systems do not treat men and women equally. They impose an unequal burden insofar as agricultural labor and fuelwood gathering are concerned, and they deny women many tenurial rights, including the right to inherit. Under these circumstances, government recognition of community-based rights, especially if institutionalized via restrictive legal instruments, can actually reinforce the gender inequalities rooted in religion, culture, and national or ethnic practice.

One example of an otherwise theoretically sound forest-management program that does not address entrenched gender inequalities is India's Joint Forest Management (JFM) Program, whose implementing resolutions either tacitly condone or reinforce a number of these inequalities. As a timber-regeneration strategy, many JFM groups have closed off local forests. But though this practice increases timber yields in typically "male" industries, it undermines womens' daily efforts to collect non-timber forest products since they are breaking the law if they even enter protected forests. With such policies in force, their only legal alternative is to walk the extra distance to a non-protected area—often a severe hardship.

Policies that limit the collection of non-timber forest products can also decrease returns on traditional "female" labor. For example, an important source of income for many women, the tendu leaf grows

Box 8. (continued)

best in direct sunlight. But effective forest "protection" cuts yields by increasing shade, thus harming women disproportionately.

On the other hand, Nepal's government has begun to address historical gender inequities in forest management. The Master Plan for the Forestry Sector of Nepal (1989) specifically articulates the objective of gaining the confidence of women, those "who actually make the daily management decisions." According to the Plan's guidelines, "one-third of the members of the users' committees should be women." (Given the incomplete nature of forest legislation policy in Nepal, it remains to be seen whether this reorientation will tangibly improve the lives of forest-dependent women.)

Even though the global trend is clearly moving toward more "equitable" arrangements, few, if any, cultural systems in South and Southeast Asia aspire to "western" or "modern" levels of equality. Indeed, calls for reform are sometimes perceived by local people as cultural imperialism and cause for hostility and resentment—even when the advocates are community members.

At best, such resentment incites dialogue and opens debate. At worst, it can lead to the rejection of otherwise sustainable management practices and the ongoing deterioration of forest resources. For this reason, gender-equalizing practices must be promoted extremely judiciously and with full sensitivity of prevailing religious and cultural norms.

Source: Madhu Sarin, "Regenerating India's Forests: Reconciling Gender Equity with Joint Forest Management." Paper prepared for the International Workshop in India's Forest Management and Ecological Revival, February 1994.

VI.
PROMOTING SUSTAINABLE FOREST MANAGEMENT THROUGH COMMUNITY-BASED TENURE

Equitable Bargaining

Both forest-dependent communities and national governments in Asia and the Pacific have obvious interests in ensuring that forest resources are sustainably managed. This report aims to promote those interests by encouraging the establishment of equitable bargaining processes. In an effective and fair process, both parties understand their rights and concomitant duties, and negotiate a mutually acceptable, secure, and balanced agreement. Both parties likewise know what their optimal outcome will be. For communities, this report concludes that the optimal outcome would be recognition of private community-based rights.

Many forest communities are uniquely positioned to help protect forests. As the guardians of national interests and resource patrimonies, national governments and their forest bureaucracies also have a vital role to play. But for too long, forest-dependent peoples and government bureaucracies have interacted poorly, if at all. Long overdue, a dialogue might result in a shared commitment to right and secure the balance between local-level community interests and national interests.

The final decision about what agreement is most appropriate in any given forest area should be shared by the community (or communities) concerned and the appropriate government agency or official. A good agreement will provide for the establishment of locally appropriate incentives that are in all parties' best long-term interests.

Community Forest Leases

Local communities would have the greatest leverage and capacity to negotiate and promote their self interest if they possessed government recognized private community-based property rights. Except in Pacific Island nation, however, few forest communities are likely to possess such leverage, at least in the short term, since political realities and prevailing interpretations of national laws in Asia largely preclude it. The only options available to many, if not most, forest-dependent communities are to lease rights or otherwise secure privileges to their local resource base or lose access.

Government leasing of rights to forest land is the core element of community forestry programs in Nepal, Thailand, and the Philippines. It also occurs, to a limited extent, in Indonesia. *Community forest leases and other rights based on privileges stem from the assumption that government owns the resources and the other party had no legal right to use them.* Essentially they are agreements between appropriate government agencies and resource-dependent communities that recognize the rights and duties of both entities. Written documents, however, are "less important than the understanding, commitment, and good faith of parties to the agreement. The process, not the paper, is the key."[141] The goal should be to provide forest-dependent people with appropriate legal and economic incentives to protect remaining natural forests and to regenerate degraded ones. Ideally, the agreements should be simple, straightforward, and reflect local variables. They especially need to discourage migration into forest areas and help stabilize populations that are already there. *(See Appendix B, Sample Community Forest Lease.)*

Before any specific agreements are reached or any community-based rights recognized or granted, communities should first identify the areas that they believe belong to them. *(See Box 9, Community Mapping Initiatives.)* Three other steps are also essential: government officials must understand how the community perceives its needs, the community must understand the nature and potential impact of the initiative proposed, and both parties must determine if prospects for community-based tenurial rights are realistic.

Box 9. Community Mapping Initiatives

Around the world, forest-dwelling communities are beginning to recognize the power that maps can have in efforts to protect their lands from intruders. Legally marginalized and politically invisible, forest dwellers have all too often been unable to effectively oppose government resettlement schemes, wealthy concessionaires, gun-wielding colonists and soldiers, and others vying for scarce land and resources. Recently, non-governmental organizations and local communities have collaborated—in efforts to enhance local rights and claims—to make precise maps of the areas inhabited by forest-dwellers to inform outsiders about their occupancy and sustainable resource-management systems. By combining locally generated sketch maps with government base maps and using a Global Positioning System (GPS)[a] to check positional accuracy, villagers can create "scientific proof" and legally cognizable evidence of their occupancy. Two of the best examples of successful mapping projects are in Latin America and Asia.

Threatened by the incursion of loggers, cattle ranchers, and the proposed Pan-American Highway, the people of eastern Panama have been organizing themselves to defend their lands. Together with the Centro de Estudios y Acción Social Panameño (CEASPA) and the Center for the Support of Native Lands, the Congresses of the Wounaan, Emberá, and Kuna led a project to map the subsistence land-use patterns of the 82 forest-dependent communities that live in the area known as the Darién. Community-generated sketch maps were combined with government maps, aerial photographs, and GPS to produce technically accurate representations of local resource use.

When the project was completed, the Darién communities presented a final composite map to government ministers and local and international non-governmental organizations during a forum on Indigenous Cultures and Resources. At this forum, the Minister of Government and Justice, who had previously authorized the use of force to suppress indigenous rights demonstrations, acknowledged the importance of the forest-dwellers' struggle. In addition, the Instituto Geográfico Nacional, which collaborated in the project, concluded that the maps generated by the forest communities were more accurate and detailed than previous maps and that it would incorporate them—indigenous names and all—into their official map of the

Box 9 (continued)

region. The final maps, still the property of the Wounaan, Kuna, and Emberá, will be used to discuss future plans for the land, including negotiations over the construction of the Pan-American Highway through the Darién Gap.

In East Kalimantan, Indonesia, the World Wide Fund for Nature (WWF)/Indonesia helped villagers conduct a similar mapping project. WWF/Indonesia and the communities involved are preparing to recommend a status change of the areas they inhabit from Nature Reserve to National Park. The change would allow them to use the land and resources in zones according to commonly agreed traditional use. A mapping method similar to that of the Panama project was used. Locally sketched maps were used as base maps, and details and corrections were made with GPS. Ultimately, the mapping team will use Geographic Information Systems (GIS, a computer program used to overlay multiple information sets) technology to help delineate zones and store biological research data.

During the village mapping exercises, the mapping team realized that participation by all groups in the community is crucial because people perceive resources according to how they use them. (Women, for example, generally want to conserve areas where medicinal plants, vegetables, rattan, and other staples of subsistence are cultivated, as well as preserving areas essential for drinking water and firewood. Men, on the other hand, are more concerned about protecting areas used for hunting and commercial purposes.[b]) In addition, villagers discovered that it was essential to include representatives from neighboring communities in their discussions in order to achieve a unified voice from the field and to avert potential conflicts of interest. Similarly, they found it useful to involve relevant government parties in the mapping process because they were distinguishing boundaries for parks, villages, and forest concessions.

Ultimately, the communities developed detailed maps showing their traditional lands zoned for various uses. For each zone, including areas outside the park boundary whose purpose is to maintain the integrity of the parklands (i.e. Buffer Zones), they devised user rights and responsibilities. These regulations cover areas ranging from strict conservation of sacred areas to Wildlife Sanctuary Zones that are closed to hunting but open to limited tourism, research, and

Box 9 (continued)

the collection of non-timber forest products. In June 1994, Forest Department officials and provincial and district governments presented the village maps to the Ministry of Forestry, recommending an official status change of the area from Nature Reserve to National Park. Even if the maps and other information gathered are not utilized by the National Government, the villagers have become politically involved—hopefully permanently.

Forest-dependent people can thus help prevent outside incursion by mapping their lands and resource use. As the above projects suggest, maps can be used to support community-level education, political unity, and allow for local participation in government conservation programs. In Darién, most of the inhabitants had only a local view of the forest destruction that is occurring on a larger scale. By bringing communities together to map their lands and discuss regional development, local people saw the destruction plaguing the entire area and got a sense of how it affects them. Working together has helped foster solidarity among the communities and made them politically stronger. Clearly, mapping can be an invaluable tool for local-level empowerment as forest-dwellers struggle to protect their lands against outside encroachment.

Notes
a. GPS is a relatively inexpensive low tech hand-held tool used in the field to determine latitude and longitude at any given point.
b. Peter Poole, "Indigenous Peoples, Mapping, and Biodiversity Conservation: A Survey of Current Activities," p. 13.

Sources: Janis Alcorn, Catherine Veninga, Derek Denniston, "Defending the Land with Maps," *World Watch* (January–February 1994). Nicanor González, Francisco Herrera, Mac Chapin, "Ethnocartography in the Darién," *Cultural Survival Quarterly* (Winter 1995). Peter Poole, "Indigenous Peoples, Mapping, and Biodiversity Conservation: A Survey of Current Activities." Bill Threlkeld. World Wide Fund for Nature (WWF)/Indonesia-Kayan Mentarang Project, "Participatory Tools for Community-Forest Profiling and Zonation of Conservation Areas, Experiences from the Kayan Mentarang Nature Reserve, East Kalimantan, Indonesia," (July 1994).

Establishing a community-based forest management project without informing local communities early on is foolhardy. Governments should carefully gauge local acceptance of or opposition to any such initiative, especially from those who primarily depend on the resources targeted. Persistent, widespread opposition should stop the project.

Information Dissemination

Before any equal bargaining process can begin, bargainers must understand their rights, duties, and options. Villagers and other forest-dependent peoples are generally less informed than government officials.

In Papua New Guinea, private community-based property rights are in effect in over 90 percent of the country. Although communication between the government and communities has been imperfect, the Natural Resources Options Network proposed by the 1992 Conservation Needs Assessment is one promising model for opening meaningful, informed dialogue in other forest-dependent communities in the six Asian countries studied, as well as elsewhere. *(See Chapter IV.)* The simple fact is that forest-dependent people make decisions daily that have impacts on the local resource base. Being better informed about the potential impacts of outside developments and about possible choices will, if nothing else, provide them with opportunities to make better decisions.

Informed Consent

Alone, dissemination of information regarding options is not enough. Those affected must give informed consent before any externally initiated community-based forest management project starts. Culturally appropriate public hearings, open to all people dependent on the area, relevant government agencies and officials, and representatives of appropriate non-governmental organizations is a good next step.

Women and other disenfranchised subgroups should not only be heard but also, if necessary, be accorded separate identities and representation in any decision-making.[142] The written results of the discussions should be publicly disseminated in a timely fashion with special attention given to any commitments made in response to local concerns. Where few are literate, a summary of the discussion should be orally disseminated.

Notice

People living in areas where community-based forest management is under consideration should receive notice before any formal initiative begins. *At a minimum,* the notice should
1. briefly describe the project;
2. be in the area's *lingua franca;*
3. contain a map of the affected area;
4. describe the proponent's proposed rights and responsibilities;
5. define the local community's current rights and responsibilities and show how they would change if the area is designated for community forestry; and,
6. inform people where and when meetings will be held locally.

Community and Legal Personalities

Working with communities (that is, with groups) to legitimize local management systems over large areas is more efficient than dealing with individuals. When negotiating tenurial rights agreements, however, it is essential to define the "community" or "user group." Who should define it is also key since some communities are ill-defined, overlap with neighboring communities, or include conflicting factions. Some follow unscrupulous leaders who will grab a disproportionate share of any project benefits.

Resolving such problems is difficult. Theoretically, people should bear primary responsibility for defining their own community or communities, but they are not always able to do so. If the number of communities is too large (and their size too small), it may be necessary for some communities to consolidate for the purposes of reaching an agreement, or revert to individual agreements.

Some forest-based communities—among them users' groups or informal organizations capable of and willing to protect a designated area of natural forest—don't have the internal cohesion and capacity to manage, sustainably develop, allocate, and enforce informal customary rights over the entire local resource base. Where they are already protecting remaining areas of natural forest, less comprehensive forest leases would legalize their efforts. *(See Appendix A, Sample Forest Protection Lease.)*

Communities wishing to enter into formal agreements or take part in commercial extraction enterprises will probably need "legal personalities," particularly if they are going to be receiving income that must be processed or taxed. The degree and rigor of requirements for creating and legally recognizing community-based institutions vary by country, but in any case requiring that they establish legal personalities by registering with a typically far-off government agency has serious drawbacks. Sometimes the legal personalities—such as non-stock, non-profit corporations in the Philippines—can be unilaterally dissolved when communities fail to comply with procedural requirements, such as filing financial statements or minutes of meetings.

A more informal approach works better. In the Indian state of West Bengal, for example, forest-protection committees simply register with their local district forest officers before entering into joint forest-management agreements.[143] This tactic is an attractive alternative to incorporation—provided that the committees' registration cannot be arbitrarily revoked by forestry officials. Unfortunately, they can be in West Bengal.

An even better procedure would be to simply require a census of all community members (or all adults or heads of households) and request that they sign the title or lease. The completed census or list of signatories could legally define the community and become an integral part of any title or lease. Either list would ensure that if the corporation is dissolved or registration were revoked, the title or lease would not revert back to the government since there would still be two parties as is required in a legally binding agreement.

Third Parties

In some areas, outside parties—particularly non-governmental organizations—have an important role to play in helping communities negotiate agreements with governments. Third-party intermediaries familiar with and trusted by members of local communities, and knowledgeable of external interests and processes, can be profoundly helpful in negotiating viable and equitable community-based tenurial arrangements. Indeed, since forest-dependent communities often lack the experience necessary to navigate diverse cultural, bureaucratic, and organizational demands and expectations, many community forestry and conservation projects probably owe their very existence to the invaluable assistance of third-party intermediaries.[144]

A troublesome question, however, is whether a third-party intermediary must be involved in negotiating the terms of community-based forest management agreements. Clearly, no blanket requirement for a third-party intermediary is appropriate since their existence and availability cannot be presumed, nor can their loyalty to local communities be assured. Requiring the involvement of intermediaries should depend on a number of factors including the particular community's degree of organization and internal cohesion, community and government preferences. When a community wants the involvement of a third-party intermediary, however, that decision should be respected.

Negotiations and Benefit Sharing

Soon after the concerned community and the state reach a preliminary agreement, formal negotiations should begin. The forest-management agreement might cover—but should not be limited to:
1. a natural resource management plan;
2. project boundaries (including internal boundaries to be managed or co-managed by various constituencies according to different plans);
3. the routes of service roads and construction details;
4. employment guarantees;
5. hunting, gathering, and farming rights; and
6. other provisions for benefit sharing including (as needed) a formula for allocating profits to communities, individuals, or the state.

An array of arrangements are possible and no set formula will succeed in every situation. Each agreement calls for case-by-case development. One recommendation is universal though: once final, all agreements should be summarized in writing, orally explained, and signed by those in agreement or their authorized leaders.[145]

The division of benefits may require share-holding agreements, representation on the corporation's board of directors, allocation of a percentage of profits from annual operations (including the criteria to determine that percentage),[146] the creation of an independently run community trust, or the construction of new facilities such as a school or health clinic that serve the community. The importance of local contributions, whether in-kind or financial, should also be kept in mind. In other words, communities that enter into agreements to protect and sustainably manage forest resources are providing a service in the public interest. They are not mere beneficiaries of government largesse, rather, they are partners in an important endeavor.

VII.
Conclusion

In many developing countries, tropical forests are the single most important natural resource for rural communities. Woodlands provide food, shelter, and fuel, often nourishing the spirits of their inhabitants as well as their bodies. Unfortunately, few national governments in developing countries recognize forest-dependent peoples' locally-based natural resource rights or their contributions to sustainable forest management. Nor do most countries give local resource users any meaningful say in decisions on national forest laws and policies. Instead, many adhere to colonially inspired and centralized systems of forest land ownership that legally disenfranchise many rural citizens.

National legal systems that benefit political and economic elites also isolate the hundreds of millions of people who inhabit or depend upon tropical forests for survival. Such systems reinforce the inequitable distribution of the benefits of natural resources. They also undermine local incentives for sustainable development and contribute to the still-accelerating rate of tropical deforestation.

Three fundamental and persistent misrepresentations are often used to marginalize forest dwellers and other forest-dependent peoples, even though they have been thoroughly disproved.[147] One is that forest-dependent peoples are few in number (outdated and inaccurate official counts underestimate the population of classified forest areas). Another is that forest-dependent peoples use public resources illegally. The third is that they are destroying the forests, especially with slash-and-burn farming.

A growing body of evidence demonstrates that many forest-dependent people actually protect biologically rich areas and sustainably manage local ecosystems. In particular, many forest-dwellers rely on elaborate systems of community-based property rights which have been developed over many generations, systems that often spring from long experience and a deep sense of obligation to the natural world.

Forest bureaucracies know, of course, that when push comes to shove many forest-dependent communities can resist or bollix governmental forest-management schemes that strike them as inequitable and unsustainable, however "legal." Traditionally marginalized peoples, including forest-dependent populations, won't allow themselves to be legislated or developed out of existence. By building partnerships with forest communities, governments can stave off potential unrest and develop an alternative strategy for sustainably managing fast-disappearing forest resources.

The plight of forest-dependent communities has been a long time in the making, as has the well-documented failure of state-managed systems. Now, the deforestation crises that many South and Southeast Asian countries face can be defused only by a fair and balanced government partnership with local communities. Both power and its rewards must be shared with forest-dependent communities, and community and national interests must be balanced to promote the common good.

National and state authorities need not, and should not, be eliminated from the management processes of forest resources. Empowering local communities does not mean disempowering governments. The states play a vital and necessary role in managing tropical forest resources, but it is one they share with forest-dependent communities and one that should be used to secure the balance between community and national interests and thereby promote both.

Only by sharing authority can overburdened national forest departments truly help communities and the nation sustainably develop and equitably share in the forest patrimony. In turn, by accepting their share of responsibility and cooperating with reasonable state regulations, local communities will be better able to promote the common good, as well as their own.

ABOUT THE AUTHORS

Owen Lynch is a Senior Associate in the Asia and Pacific Program at the World Resources Institute's Center for International Development and Environment, where he works primarily on community-based resources management and law issues. He also lectures at the Johns Hopkins University School of Advanced International Studies on environmental issues in developing countries. Previously, he taught for seven years at the University of the Philippines College of Law. He has a Juris Doctor from The Catholic University and a Doctor of Laws and Master of Laws degrees from Yale Law School.

Kirk Talbott is a Senior Associate and the Regional Director for the Asia and Pacific Program at the World Resources Institute's Center for International Development and Environment, where he works on environmental strategies, laws, and policies in Asia, Africa, and the Caribbean. Previously, he practiced International Law in Washington, DC and conducted research on indigenous knowledge of ecosystem management for the United Nations University. After graduating from Yale University, he earned a Masters Degree in International Relations and a Juris Doctor from Georgetown University.

APPENDICES

APPENDIX A. Sample Forest Protection Lease

This agreement, dated _____, is made and entered into between the_____, represented by the
                [national government]

_____, referred to as the
    [appropriate government agency official]

GRANTOR, and the _____, whose members have
                 [local community]

signed this Agreement

[and/or]

are identified in the attached census,

which forms an integral part of this Agreement. They have formed themselves into the _____, hereinafter
              [name of community entity]

referred to as the GRANTEE.

WHEREAS, the GRANTOR has legal authority under

_____ of _____
[appropriate section]   [appropriate legislative act]

to enter into agreements with forest managers which grants them legal rights to exploit and reside on classified forest land;

WHEREAS, the GRANTEE is qualified to enter into a lease agreement with the _____ and
[appropriate government agency/official]
has applied to do so; and

WHEREAS, the GRANTOR has evaluated and favorably considered the application of the GRANTEE:

NOW, THEREFORE, in consideration of the foregoing premises and the following terms and conditions, the GRANTOR and the GRANTEE, of their own free volition, enter into this FOREST LEASE, which covers an area located in_____

_____, District of _____,

Province of _____, containing an area of

_____ hectares and technically described in the attached map, which is an integral part of this Agreement.

* * * *

Terms and Conditions

GRANTEE

1. The GRANTEE shall have the sole and exclusive right peacefully to utilize, manage, and protect the land and natural resources located within the area described above against any third parties.

2. The GRANTEE shall preserve monuments and other landmarks within the confines of the land that designate corners and boundaries.

3. The GRANTEE shall protect and conserve the forest trees and forest products naturally grown on the land and shall

cooperate with the _____
[appropriate government agency/official]
in an effort to protect forest areas immediately adjacent to the leased area.

4. The GRANTEE shall not cut, gather, or harvest for commercial use naturally grown forest products from the area or any adjacent area except in accordance with a license or permit that shall be issued by the GRANTOR upon prior application of the GRANTEE.

GRANTOR

1. The GRANTOR shall extend technical assistance, extension services, and other support to the GRANTEE.

2. The GRANTOR shall maintain the present legal status of the area and shall not reclassify or grant to any and all third parties rights or privileges to develop, utilize, or manage the area during the existence of this Agreement.

3. The GRANTOR shall, upon the request of the GRANTEE, assist efforts to protect the area from encroachment and any unauthorized extraction of natural resources.

4. The GRANTOR shall not terminate or cancel this Agreement unless the GRANTEE fails to comply with the terms and conditions of the Agreement within one year after being notified in writing of the alleged violations.

The provisions in this Agreement have been explained by the GRANTOR in a language understandable to the GRANTEE prior to the signing of the Agreement.

This Agreement becomes effective upon its signing by the

authorized parties and shall continue for a period of _____ years, renewable for another _____ years at the option of the GRANTEE.

    IN WITNESS WHEREOF, the parties have signed their names

below this _____ day of _____, _____.

_____   _____
[Community Representative of   [Official]
Corporation/Cooperative]

        _____
           [Representative of the User
          Group or Informal Organization]

Signed in the presence of

_____   _____
      [witness]   [witness]

APPENDIX B. Sample Forest Community Lease

This Agreement, dated _____, is made and entered into between the _____, represented by the
[national government]

_____, referred to as the
[appropriate government agency official]

GRANTOR, and the community of _____, whose
[local community]

members have

signed this Agreement

[and/or]

are identified in the attached census,

which forms an integral part of this Agreement. They have formed

themselves into the _____, hereinafter
[name of users' group]

referred to as the GRANTEE.

WHEREAS, the GRANTOR has legal authority under

_____ of _____
[appropriate section]   [appropriate legislative act]

to enter into agreements with forest managers that grants them legal rights to extract from and reside on classified forest land;

WHEREAS, the GRANTEE is qualified to enter into a lease agreement with the GRANTOR and has applied to do so; and

WHEREAS, the GRANTOR has evaluated and favorably considered the application of the GRANTEE:

NOW, THEREFORE, in consideration of the foregoing premises and the following terms and conditions, the GRANTOR and the GRANTEE, of their own free volition, enter into this COMMUNITY FOREST LEASE, which covers an area located

in_____

_____, District of _____,

Province of _____, containing an area of

_____ hectares and technically described in the attached map, which is an integral part of this Agreement.

* * * *

Terms and Conditions

GRANTEE

1. The GRANTEE shall have the sole and exclusive right peacefully to possess, occupy, manage, and protect the land and natural resources located within the area described above against any and all third parties.

2. The GRANTEE shall preserve monuments and other landmarks within the confines of the land that designate corners and boundaries.

3. The GRANTEE shall protect and conserve the forest trees and forest products naturally grown on the land and shall

cooperate with the _____
_____ [appropriate government agency/official]
in an effort to protect forest areas immediately adjacent to the leased area.

4. The GRANTEE shall not cut, gather, or harvest for commercial use naturally grown forest products from the area or any adjacent area except in accordance with a license or permit issued by the GRANTOR upon prior application of the GRANTEE.

5. The GRANTEE shall be able to cut, gather, or harvest for commercial use trees or other forest products that are planted or otherwise grown by its members.

6. The GRANTEE, by entering into this Agreement shall not be deemed to have waived any claim of preexisting or prospective private ownership rights inside or outside the area covered by this Agreement.

GRANTOR

1. The GRANTOR shall extend technical assistance, extension services, and other support to the GRANTEE.

2. The GRANTOR shall maintain the present legal status of the area and shall not reclassify or grant to any and all third parties any rights or privileges to develop, utilize, or manage the area during the existence of this Agreement.

3. The GRANTOR shall, upon the request of the GRANTEE, assist efforts to protect the area from encroachment and any unauthorized extraction of natural resources.

4. The GRANTOR shall not terminate or cancel this Agreement unless the GRANTEE fails to comply with the terms and conditions of the Agreement within one year after being notified in writing of the alleged violations.

The provisions in this Agreement have been explained by the GRANTOR in a language understandable to the GRANTEE prior to the signing of the Agreement.

This Agreement becomes effective upon its signing by the

authorized parties and shall continue for a period of _____

years, renewable for another _____ years at the option of the GRANTEE.

IN WITNESS WHEREOF, the parties have signed their names

below this _____ day of _____, _____.

[Community Representative of Corporation/Cooperative]

[Official]

Signed in the presence of

[witness]

[witness]

NOTES

1. Quoted in Madhav Gadgil et al., *"Draft Background Notes for the Committee on National Forest Policy and Forest (Conservation) Act,"* (unpublished manuscript (dated 1989) on file at the Centre for Science and Environment in New Delhi), 39.
2. Mark Poffenberger, ed., *Keepers of the Forest: Land Management Alternatives in Southeast Asia* (West Hartford, Conn.: Kumarian Press, 1989), 19.
3. Data taken from World Resources Institute, in collaboration with the United Nations Environment Programme and the United Nations Development Programme, *World Resources 1994–1995: A Guide to the Global Environment* (New York: Oxford University Press, 1994), 86.
4. Figures taken from Charles V. Barber, Nels C. Johnson, and Emmy Hafild, *Breaking the Logjam: Obstacles to Forest Policy Reform in Indonesia and the United States* (Washington, D.C.: World Resources Institute, 1994), 4–5.
5. For a detailed discussion of the causes and ramifications of this natural disaster, *see* Pinkaew Leungaramsri and Noel Rajesh, eds., *The Future of People and Forests in Thailand After the Logging Ban* (Bangkok: Project for Ecological Recovery, 1992).
6. For a detailed discussion of the causes of this natural disaster, *see* Marites Danguilan Vitug, *The Politics of Logging: Power from the Forest* (Manila: Philippine Center for Investigative Journalism, 1993).
7. "Huge Toll from South Asia Floods Tied to Environmental Degradation," *The Christian Science Monitor*, July 29, 1993: 1; and Binod Bhattarai, "Worse Floods in Living Memory Claim Hundreds of Lives," *Inter Press Service*, July 29, 1993. It must be

noted, however, that some analysts are not convinced that deforestation was the primary cause of these floods. Citing the inherent geological instability of the Himalayas, they contend that slumpage and mass wasting are inevitable and that floods are a regular occurrence in this part of the world: those that occurred in the summer of 1993 just happened to be worse than usual.
8. International Tropical Timber Organization (ITTO), *Tropical Forest Management Update,* June 1993, vol. 3, no. 3:10–12.
9. William Ascher, *Communities and Sustainable Forestry in Developing Countries* (San Francisco: Institute for Contemporary Studies Press, 1995), 11.
10. For a systematic presentation and refutation of these stereotypes, *see* Owen J. Lynch, *Whither the People? Demographic, Tenurial, and Agricultural Aspects of the Tropical Forestry Action Plan, Issues in Development* (Washington, D.C.: World Resources Institute, 1990).
11. Barber et al., 1994, *see* note 4.
12. Norani Visetbhakdi, "Deforestation and Reforestation in Thailand," *Bangkok Bank Monthly Review,* June 1989:243; and Pisit na Patalung, private communication, November, 1990.
13. World Bank, *Philippines Environment and Natural Resource Management Study* (Washington, D.C.: The World Bank, 1989), ix.
14. Robert Repetto, *The Forest for the Trees?: Government Policies and the Misuse of Forest Resources* (Washington, D.C.: World Resources Institute, 1988), 17–23.
15. For more detailed discussions of the dynamics of deforestation, *see,* e.g., Nels Johnson and Bruce Cabarle, *Surviving the Cut: Natural Forest Management in the Humid Tropics* (Washington, D.C.: World Resources Institute, 1993); and Maria Concepcion Cruz, Carrie A. Meyer, Robert Repetto, and Richard Woodward, *Population Growth, Poverty, and Environmental Stress: Frontier Migration in the Philippines and Costa Rica* (Washington, D.C.: World Resources Institute, 1992).
16. Lynch, 1990, *see* note 10.
17. *See* Cruz et al., 1992, *see* note 15.
18. United Nations Conference on Environment and Development Report, 1991, 61. The loss of biodiversity, by contrast, was

blamed on the national policies that promote and subsidize the clearing of land for agriculture. United Nations Conference on Environment and Development Report, 1991, 63.
19. Cruz et al., 1992, 25–28, *see* note 15; Yongwuth Chalamwong and Gershon Feder, *Land Ownership Security and Land Values in Rural Thailand*, World Bank Staff Working Papers No. 790 (Washington, D.C.: The World Bank, 1986); and William C. Thiesenhusen, "Implications of the Rural Land Tenure System for the Environmental Debate: Three Scenarios," *The Journal of Developing Areas* 26 (October 1991):1.
20. This shortcoming is prevalent in most countries with tropical forests. Lynch, 1990, *see* note 10.
21. Though the transmigration program was initiated in 1905, a full one-third of the total number of resettlements took place in the two year period 1984–1986 as part of the Third Five-Year Plan. The World Conservation Union (IUCN), N. Mark Collins, Jeffrey A. Sayer, Timothy C. Whitmore, eds., *The Conservation Atlas of Tropical Forests, Asia and the Pacific* (London and Basingstoke: Macmillan Press Ltd., 1991), 36–37.
22. *See*, e.g., Michael R. Dove, "Theories of Swidden Agriculture and the Political Economy of Ignorance," *Agroforestry Systems* (The Hague: Martinus Nighoff, 1983) 1:85–99, and Katherine Warner, *Shifting Cultivators: Local Technical Knowledge and Natural Resource Management in the Humid Tropics* (Rome: Food and Agriculture Organization, 1991).
23. This insight was first published by the FAO in 1957 in a book written by Harold Conklin, *Hanunoo Agriculture: A Report on an Integral System of Shifting Cultivation in the Philippines* (Rome: Food and Agriculture Organization of the United Nations (FAO). For more recent insights, *see* Katherine Warner. *Shifting Cultivators: Local Technical Knowledge and Natural Resource Management in the Humid Tropics.* Rome: Food and Agriculture Organization of the United Nations, 1991; Janis B. Alcorn, "Indigenous Agroforestry Strategies Meeting Farmers' Needs," in Anthony Anderson, ed. *Alternatives to Deforestation: Steps Toward Sustainable Use of the Amazon Rain Forest* (New York: Columbia University Press, 1990); Julie Denslow and Christine Padoch, eds., *People of the Tropical Rain Forest* (Berkeley: University of

California Press, 1988); S. C. Chin, "Do Shifting Cultivators Deforest?" *Forest Resources in the Third World* (Penang, Malaysia: Sahabat Alam Malaysia, 1987); Jaganath Pathy, "Shifting Cultivators of India: Bearing the Brunt of Development" *Forest Resources in the Third World*; Michael Dove, *Swidden Agriculture in Indonesia: The Subsistence Strategies of the Kalimantan Kantu'* (Berlin: Mouton Press, 1985); *Swidden Cultivation in Asia*, 3 Vols. (Bangkok: UNESCO Regional Office, 1983); Michael Dove, "Swidden Agriculture and the Political Economy of Ignorance," *Agroforestry Systems* (The Hague: Martinus Nighoff, I:85–99, 1983); Harold Olafson, ed., *Adaptive Strategies and Change in Philippine Swidden-based Societies* (Los Baños, Philippines: Forestry Research Institute, 1981); Terry Grandstaff, *Shifting Cultivation in Northern Thailand* (Tokyo: United Nations University, 1980); Joseph Weinstock, "Land Tenure Practices of the Swidden Cultivators of Borneo," master's thesis, Cornell University, 1979; Peter Kunstadter, E. C. Chapman, and Sanga Sabhasri, *Farmers in the Forest: Economic Development and Marginal Agriculture in Northern Thailand* (Honolulu: University of Hawaii Press, 1978); and J. E. Spencer, *Shifting Cultivation in Southeast Asia* (Berkeley: University of California Press, 1966).

24. For examples, *see* David Western and R. Michael Wright, eds., *Natural Connections: Perspectives in Community-based Conservation* (Washington, D.C. and Covel, CA: Island Press, 1994).

25. This process was the basis of Garrett Hardin's famous treatise, "The Tragedy of the Commons," which postulated that such situations are promoted when community-based resource management systems are delegitimized and states fail to manage the resource. When community-based tenure is weakened, sustainable production is often undermined and falls victim to the race for short-term gain by anyone and everyone. In effect, public land and other public resources belong to no one in particular and thus to everyone in general.

26. The distinction is important and the need for a standardized use of the term is highlighted in David Western, et al. eds., *Natural Connections: New Perspectives in Community-Based Conservation* (Washington, D.C.: Island Press, 1994). Of twelve case

studies presented in the book, only one was actually initiated and directed by the local community involved. This is not to criticize the authors or the experiences they described and analyzed. Rather, it is an effort to promote a limitation on the use of the term "community-based."

27. *See*, e.g., Michael Dove, "Government Perceptions of Traditional Social Forestry in Indonesia: The History, Causes and Implications of State Policy on Swidden Agriculture," *Community Forestry: Socioeconomic Aspects*, (Rome: Food and Agriculture Organization of the United Nations (FAO), 1985); and J.E. Spencer, *Shifting Cultivation in Southeast Asia* (Berkeley: University of California Press, 1966).

28. For an extended discussion of the dynamics of community-based resource management, *see* Margery L. Oldfield and Janis B. Alcorn, eds., *Biodiversity: Culture, Conservation, and Ecodevelopment* (Boulder, CO: Westview Press, 1991).

29. For more detailed discussion, *see* Owen J. Lynch and Janis B. Alcorn, "Tenurial Rights and Community-based Conservation," in David Western and R. Michael Wright, eds., *Natural Connections: Perspectives in Community-based Conservation* (Washington, D.C. and Covelo, CA: Island Press, 1994), 373–392.

30. Elinor Ostrom, *Governing the Commons: The Evolution of Institutions for Collective Action* (Cambridge: Cambridge University Press, 1990).

31. *See*, e.g., Nancy Peluso, *Rich Forests, Poor People and Development: Forest Access Control and Resistance in Java* (Berkeley: University of California Press, 1994); Louise Fortmann and John W. Bruce, *Whose Trees?: Proprietary Dimensions of Forestry* (Boulder, CO: Westview Press, 1988); and Barber et al., 1994, *see* note 4.

32. Boyce Rensberger, "Out of Africa 1.8 Million Years Ago? 'Java Man' Fossils Older then Thought," *The Washington Post*, Feb. 24, 1994, A4.

33. R. L. Winzeler, "Ecology, Culture, Social Organization and State Formation in Southeast Asia," *Current Anthropology*, 1976, vol. 17, no. 4:624.

34. D.G.E. Hall, *A History of South-East Asia, Fourth Edition* (New York: St. Martin's Press, 1981), 236–238.

35. Wilhelm G. Solheim II, "New Light on a Forgotten Past," *National Geographic*, March 1971, vol. 139, no. 3:330–339.
36. Hall, 1981, 236–238, *see* note 34.
37. For a discussion of the history of forest depletion in England, *see* Chapter 10, "England," in John Perlin, *A Forest Journey: The Role of Wood in the Development of Civilization* (New York and London: W.W. Norton & Company, 1989), 163–245.
38. J. Ball, *Indonesian Legal History* (Sydney: Oughtershaw Press, 1982), 116–117.
39. Proclamations of May 3, 1800 and October 3, 1801, applying to the maritime provinces.
40. Government of Sri Lanka (GOSL), *Report of the Land Commission*, 1987 (Colombo: Sri Lanka: Department of Government Printing, 1990), Section 5.14.
41. The state originally gave *birta* lands to an individual as a reward for bravery, especially in military action. *Birta* lands subsequently came to include any state-granted territory that was exempt from land taxes. *Source:* Mahesh C. Regmi, *Land Tenure and Taxation in Nepal*, Bibliotheca Himalayica Series 1, vol. 26 (Kathmandu: Ratna Pustak Bhandar, 1978), 348.
42. Ibid.
43. Nicholas P. Cushner, *Landed Estates in the Colonial Philippines* (New Haven: Yale University Southeast Asia Studies, 1976), 68.
44. John L. Phelan, *The Hispanization of the Philippines: Spanish Aims and Filipino Responses* (Madison: University of Wisconsin Press, 1959), 94.
45. Emma H. Blair and James A. Robertson, eds., *The Philippine Islands, 1493–1898* (Mandaluyong, Philippines: Cachos Hermanos, 1903–09, 1973 edition), vol. 34:249.
46. Ibid., vol. 34:302–3.
47. Carl C. Plehn, "Taxation in the Philippines," *Political Science Quarterly*, 1901–02, vol. 16:680–711 and vol. 17:125–48.
48. Blair and Robertson, 1903–09, vol. 51:182–273, *see* note 45.
49. Karl J. Pelzer, *Pioneer Settlement in the Asiatic Tropics: Studies in Land Utilization and Agricultural Colonization in Southeast Asia* (New York: American Geographical Society, 1945), 90; and David R. Sturtevant, *Popular Uprisings in the Philippines, 1840–1940* (Ithaca: Cornell University Press, 1976), 37.

50. For a fascinating analysis of the political and economic origins of the Spanish-American War *see* Luzviminda Bartolome Francisco and Jonathan Shepard Fast, *Conspiracy for Empire: Big Business, Corruption and the Politics of Imperialism in America 1876–1907* (Quezon City, Philippines: Foundation for National Studies, 1985).
51. For more detailed discussion, *see* Owen J. Lynch, *Colonial Legacies in a Fragile Republic: A History of Philippine Land Law and State Formation with Emphasis on the Early U.S. Regime (1898–1913)*, J.S.D. (Doctor of Laws) dissertation, Yale University Law School, 1992.
52. Philip Hirsch, "Forests, Forest Preserves, and Forest Land in Thailand," *The Geographical Journal*, 1989, vol. 156, no. 2:166–74. These local leaders were described as feudal chiefs whose "forests were recognized, in general, as properties to be maintained...and passed on to their heirs. According to the property rights of the day, the chiefs allowed concessionaires to exploit the teak forests. The deterioration of the forests was evident and disputes among the concessionaires were widespread." Thailand Development Research Institute (TDRI), *Thailand Natural Resources Profile: Is the Resource Base for Thailand's Development Sustainable?* (Bangkok: Thailand Development Research Institute, 1987), 83.
53. There is considerable confusion as to when, and pursuant to what law, the claim was made. Amara Pongsapich cited Ministry of Justice Document 74/3425 and wrote that "the first land law" promulgated on April 1, 1892, indicated that "all land belonged to the King." Amara Pongsapich, *Action Plan for a Private Tree Farm Development Program, Thailand: A Socio-Commercial Approach, Socio-Economic Aspects, Annex 10* (Bangkok: PACMAR, Inc., (in association with A&R Consultants), 1989), 5. Other studies cited 1899 as the year. TDRI (Thailand Development Research Institute), *Thailand Natural Resources Profile: Is the Resource Base for Thailand's Development Sustainable?* (Bangkok: Thailand Development Research Institute, 1987), 83; and Lert Chuntanaparb and Henry I. Wood, *Management of Degraded Forest Land in Thailand* (Bangkok: Kesetsart University, 1986), 79.

54. Thailand Development Research Institute (TDRI), *Thailand Natural Resources Profile: Is the Resource Base for Thailand's Development Sustainable?* (Bangkok: Thailand Development Research Institute, 1987), 83.
55. Toru Yano, "Land Tenure in Thailand," *Asian Survey*, 1968, vol. 8, no. 10:853.
56. Daniel Bromley, "Property Relations and Economic Development: The Other Land Reform," *World Development*, 1989, vol. 17, no. 6:867–877.
57. Sandra Moniaga, "Towards Community-Based Forestry and Recognition of Adat Property Rights in the Outer Islands of Indonesia: A Legal and Policy Analysis" in Jefferson Fox, ed., Legal Frameworks for Forest Management in Asia: Case Studies of Community/State Relations, (Honolulu, East-West Center), 1993, 131–150. Abdurrahman, *Hukum Adat Menurut Perundang Undangan Republik Indonesia* (Customary Law According to the Legal System of the Republic of Indonesia) (Jakarta: Cendana Press, 1984); and I. Sudiyat, *Hukum Adat* (Customary Law) (Yogyakarta, Indonesia: Liberty, 1981).
58. Abdurrahman, 1984, and I. Sudiyat, 1981, *see* note 57.
59. Charles V. Barber and G. Churchill, *Land Policy in Irian Jaya: Issues and Strategies* (Jakarta: Government of Indonesia/United Nations Development Programme, 1987).
60. Peraturan Pemerintah No. 21/1970 tentang Hak Pengusahaan Hutan dan Hak Pemungutan Hasil Hutan [Government Regulation No. 21/1970 concerning the Right of Forest Exploitation and the Right to Harvest Forest Products].
61. Charles V. Barber, "The Legal and Regulatory Framework for Forest Production in Indonesia" (included as Appendix 1) in Charles Zerner, *Legal Options for the Indonesian Forestry Sector* (Jakarta: Government of Indonesia/United Nations Food and Agriculture Organization, 1990).
62. A. H. Pramono, *A Brief Review on Forest Land Use and Deforestation in Indonesia* (Jakarta: Wahana Lingkungan Hidup Indonesia (WALHI), 1991); and Regional Physical Planning Programme for Transmigration (RePPProT), *The Land Resources of Indonesia* (Jakarta: Overseas Development Administration (UK) and Department of Transmigration (Indonesia), 1990).

63. Government of Indonesia, *Biodiversity Action Plan for Indonesia* (Jakarta: Ministry of National Development Planning/National Development Planning Agency, 1991).
64. Sections 14 and 31.
65. The 1985 law also provided for a proportional system of land subclassification. Fifteen percent of the kingdom's total land area was to be subclassified as conservation or protection forests. Conservation forests include forest reserves that have been designated as wildlife sanctuaries or national parks, entities that contain most of the kingdom's remaining forests. By 1988, more than 20 million hectares, or 40 percent of the kingdom's total land mass, had been designated as "forest reserves." Amara Pongsapich, "Action Plan for a Private Tree Farm Development Program, Thailand: A Socio-Commercial Approach," *Socio-Economic Aspects*, 1989, Annex 10, Table 10.6 (citing Royal Forestry Department statistics).
66. There were also 31 wildlife sanctuaries encompassing a total of 2,470,054 hectares and 59 national parks covering a total of 3,041,599 hectares. An additional 22 parks, covering 1,136,543 hectares, were pending approval. If the National Forestry Policy was to be fully implemented, however, an additional 1,048,566 more hectares would need to be designated as conservation forests.
67. Newspaper accounts of the opposition and eventual abandonment of the eviction can be found in "Villagers Protest Land Resettlement Programme," *The Bangkok Post*, April 26, 1992; Ploenpoch Varanien, "Land Resettlement Compromise Reached," *The Bangkok Post*, July 17, 1992; and Ann Danaiya Usher, "Huay Kaew: Broken Promises," *The Nation*, September 20, 1991.
68. Social Research Institute of Chiangmai University, Research and Development Institute of Khon Kaen University, Non-Governmental Organization Co-ordinating Committee on Rural Development (NGO-CORD), Northern and Northeastern Chapters, and Local Development Institute. *Community Forestry: Declaration of the Customary Rights of Local Communities: Thai Democracy at the Grassroots*, Results of the "Community Forestry in Thailand: Development Perspectives" workshop,

held at the Women Studies Center of the Social Sciences Faculty, Chiangmai University, June 27–28, 1992. (mimeo), Paragraph 16.4 (p. 26).
69. Ministry of Agriculture and Cooperatives Royal Forest Department, *Thai Forestry Master Plan*, vol. 5:85 (Bangkok), 1993.
70. Philippine Department of Environment and Natural Resources (DENR), *Philippine Forestry Statistics, 1993* (Quezon City: Forest Management Bureau, 1994).
71. The Word Bank, *Philippines: Environmental and Natural Resource Management Study* (Washington, D.C.: The World Bank, 1989), ix.
72. Maria Concepcion Cruz, Imelda Zosa-Feranil, and Cristela L. Goce, *Population Pressure and Migration: Implications for Upland Development in the Philippines*, Working Paper No. 86-06, Center for Policy and Development Studies (Los Baños: University of the Philippines at Los Baños, 1986), 12–13.
73. Maria Concepcion Cruz, private communication, March 10, 1995.
74. "Tribes to Get Ancestral Lands," *The Manila Chronicle*, November 24, 1988:8.
75. Presidential Decree No. 705, Section 15 declares that "[n]o land of the public domain 18% in slope or over shall be classified as alienable and disposable." Additional criteria in Section 16 preclude the alienable and disposable label for areas less than 18% in slope which are "...less than 250 hectares and far from or not contiguous with any certified alienable and disposable land." Alienable and disposable certification was also prohibited for areas previously proclaimed by the President as forest reserves.
76. If it was addressing a serious environmental concern, the 45% figure would presumably apply on an island-to-island, as opposed to an archipelagic, basis. As of 1995, however, more than 75% of the islands of Bohol, Basilan, Cebu, and Negros were identified for classification as agricultural and certification as alienable and disposable. On the other hand, more than half of the total land area in provinces with high concentrations of indigenous occupants was identified for classification as permanent forest. These provinces include Agusan del Sur, Ifugao, Mountain, Kalinga-Apayao, and Occidental Mindoro. Philip-

pine Department of Environment and Natural Resources (DENR), *Philippine Forestry Statistics, 1993* (Quezon City: Forest Management Bureau, 1994).
77. The World Bank, *Philippines: Environment and Natural Resource Management Study* (Washington, D.C.: The World Bank, 1989), 10 (Paragraph 2.4). In Paragraph 2.2 the study noted that "of the area presently classified as A&D land, it appears that at least 13% and, according to some recent estimates, perhaps 35% has slopes in excess of 18%. Conversely, as much as 28% of Forest Lands is estimated to have slopes under 18%, although much of this is found at higher altitudes."
78. Ibid.
79. Ibid., 86, paragraph 6.5.
80. Philippine Presidential Decree No. 1998 (1985).
81. Government of Sri Lanka (GOSL), *Natural Resources of Sri Lanka: Conditions and Trends*, A Report Prepared for the Natural Resources, Energy, and Science Authority of Sri Lanka (Colombo, Sri Lanka: Keells Business Systems, Ltd., 1991), 53.
82. Ibid., 53. In 1981 the United Nations Food and Agriculture Organization reported that the 3.5 percent annual rate of deforestation was the highest in Asia, except for Nepal. The higher deforestation estimate was made by World Resources Institute, in collaboration with The United Nations Environment Programme and The United Nations Development Programme, *World Resources 1992–93*, (New York: Oxford University Press, 1992), 287.
83. Government of Sri Lanka (GOSL), *Natural Resources of Sri Lanka: Conditions and Trends*, A Report Prepared for the Natural Resources, Energy, and Sciences authority of Sri Lanka (Colombo, Sri Lanka: Keells Business System, Ltd., 1991), 59–62.
84. GOSL (Government of Sri Lanka), *Report of the Land Commission, 1987, see* note 38, Paragraph 5.21.
85. Government of Sri Lanka, 1991, 102 and 198, *see* note 82. This estimate was made in 1984 by the Land Division of the Irrigation Department. The total area under *chena* cultivation is believed to have increased since then.
86. Ibid., 61 and 63 respectively. The loss of biodiversity, by contrast, was blamed on the national policies that promote and subsidize the clearing of land for agriculture.

87. Forest Ordinance, Sections 6 and 7. Similar prohibitions are found in the Fauna and Flora Protection Ordinance of 1938 (Sections 3 to 10).
88. Government of Gujurat, *Gujurat Forest Manual, Volume III: Forest Rights, Privileges, Concessions and Cognate Matters* (Ahmedabad: Government of Gujurat Press, 1979), 20.
89. Robert Chambers, N.C. Saxena, and Tushaan Shah, *To the Hands of the Poor: Water and Trees* (Boulder, CO: Westview Press, 1989), 148.
90. Mark Poffenberger, "The Resurgence of Community Forest Management in the Jungle Mahals of West Bengal" (presented to the Conference on South Asia's Changing Environment, Bolagio, Italy, March 16–20, 1992).
91. *See* V. Dhagamvar, "Rehabilitation: Policy and Institutional Changes Required," in Walter Fernandes and Enakshi Ganguli Thakral, eds., *Development, Displacement and Rehabilitation* (New Delhi: Indian Social Institute, 1989).
92. B. D. Sharma, *29th Report of the Commissioner for Scheduled Castes and Scheduled Tribes (1989)* (Fardiabad: Government of India Press, 1990), 108–9.
93. *See* A. L. Joshi, "Nationalization of Forest in Nepal: Why Was It Needed?," *The Nepal Journal of Forestry*, October 1991, vol. VII, no. 1:13–15.
94. *See*, e.g., Shantam S. Khadka and Surya K. Gurung, *Popular Management of Forest Resources in Selected Districts of Selected Zone: Review of Laws and Regulations on Forestry User Groups* (Kathmandu, Nepal: Centre for Economic Development and Administration, Tribhuvan University, 1990); and Deepak Bajracharya, "Deforestation in the Food/Fuel Context, Historical and Political Perspective from Nepal," *Mountain Research and Development*, 1983, vol. 3, no. 3.
95. *See*, e.g., Michel Pimbert and Jules N. Pretty, *Parks, People and Professionals: Putting "Participation" into Protected Area Management* (Geneva, United Nations Research Institute for Social Development, 1995). Michael Wells and Katrina Brandon, *Parks and People* (Washington, D.C.: The World Bank, 1992); G. Borrini, *Enhancing People's Participation in the Tropical Forests Action Programme* (Bangkok: Food and Agriculture Organiza-

tion of the United Nations (FAO), 1993); and P. Eaton, *Land Tenure and Conservation: Protected Areas in the South Pacific* (Noumea, New Caledonia: South Pacific Commission, 1985).
96. The importance of incentives, particularly tenurial incentives for indigenous peoples has been highlighted in many recent studies. *See*, e.g., Alan T. Durning, "Supporting Indigenous Peoples," in Lester R. Brown et al., *State of the World 1993: A Worldwatch Institute Report on Progress Toward a Sustainable Society* (New York and London: W. W. Norton and Company, 1993); Jefferson Fox, Owen Lynch, Mark Zimsky, and Erin Moore, eds., *Voices from the Field: Fourth Annual Social Forestry Writing Workshop* (Honolulu: East-West Center, 1992); Owen J. Lynch and Kirk Talbott, "Legal Responses to the Philippine Deforestation Crises," *Journal of International Law and Politics, 1988*, vol. 20, no. 3 (New York: New York University Press, 1988); Peter Poole, *Developing a Partnership of Indigenous Peoples, Conservationists, and Land Use Planners in Latin America*, a World Bank Policy, Planning, and Research Working Paper (Washington, D.C.: The World Bank, 1989); Shelton H. Davis, *Indigenous Peoples, Environmental Protection and Sustainable Development* (Gland, Switzerland: International Union for the Conservation of Nature and Natural Resources (IUCN), 1988); and Shelton H. Davis and Alaka Wali, *Indigenous Territories and Tropical Forest Management in Latin America*, a Policy, Planning, and Research Working Paper #1100 (Washington, D.C.: The World Bank, 1993).
97. Derived from data in World Resources Institute, in collaboration with the United Nations Environment Programme and the United Nations Development Programme, *World Resources Report 1994–95* (New York: Oxford University Press, 1994), 268 and 284.
98. World Resources Institute and the International Institute for Environment and Development, *World Resources 1986* (Washington, D.C.: World Resources Institute, 1986), Table 2.1, p. 237.
99. *National Forest Policy, 1988* (reprinted in Society for the Promotion of Wastelands Development, *Joint Forest Management Update* (New Delhi: Society for the Promotion of Wastelands Development, 1993).

100. Madhu Sarin, *From Conflicts to Collaboration: Local Institutions in Joint Forest Management*, Joint Forest Management Working Paper No. 14 (New Delhi: National Support Group for Joint Forest Management, Society for Promotion of Wastelands Development and The Ford Foundation, 1993).
101. For a more complete discussion of the history and current status of community forestry legislation in Nepal, *see* Kirk Talbott and Shantam Khadka, "Handing it Over: An Analysis of the Legal and Policy Framework of Community Forestry in Nepal," *Issues in Development* (Washington, D.C.: World Resources Institute, 1994).
102. *See*. e.g., Michael R. Dove, *Foresters' Beliefs About Farmers: A Priority for Social Science Research in Social Forestry* (Honolulu: East-West Center, 1991); and Lynch, note 10.
103. The Integrated Social Forestry Program was launched by Presidential Letter of Instruction No. 1260, dated July 28, 1982. The letter instructed the then Ministry of Natural Resources and other concerned government bureaucracies to establish a program that included a leasehold component for all citizens who resided within the "public" forest zone on or before December 31, 1981.
104. The Forest Land Management Agreement is a follow-through of the Contract Reforestation Program, funded chiefly by the Asian Development Bank. It is implemented under Department of Environment and Natural Resources Administrative Order No. 71, series 1990, as amended. Its parent regulation is the Contract Reforestation rules of Department of Environment and Natural Resources Administrative Order No. 31, series 1988. For a contractor to acquire a Forest Land Management Agreement, he is required to show that an area, formerly subjected to tree plantation activities under the Community Forestry Program, is fully planted and that 80% of the trees planted are surviving.
105. *See* Department of Environment and Natural Resources Administrative Order No. 2 of 1993.
106. Republic Act No. 7586 was approved on June 1, 1992. The Implementing Regulation is Department of Environment and Natural Resources Administrative Order No. 25, series of 1992.

107. Sec. 1, Article I, of the Department of Environment and Natural Resources Administrative Order No. 02, series of 1993.
108. Christian Erni, "Mangyan Reject National Park: What Went Wrong with IPAS on Mindoro?," *International Working Group on Indigenous Affairs Newsletter* (July/August/September 1993).
109. Legal Rights and Natural Resources Center—Kasama sa Kalikasan/Friends of the Earth—Philippines (LRC-KSK), *Ancestral Domain Rights and the IFP* (Quezon City, Philippines: LRC-KSK, 1995).
110. Legal Rights and Natural Resources Center—Kasama sa Kalikasan/Friends of the Earth—Philippines (LRC-KSK), *From Timber License Agreements to Sustainable Forest Agreements: Continuing Unsustainability and Inequity in Philippine Forest Policy, A Special Report* (Quezon City, Philippines: LRC-KSK, 1995).
111. Disathat Rojanalak, "Concrete Jungle on Forest Reserve Dilemma for Authorities," *The Bangkok Post*, November 11, 1990.
112. Kamon Pragtong and David E. Thomas, "Evolving Management Systems in Thailand," in Mark Poffenberger, ed., *Keepers of the Forest: Land Management Alternatives in Southeast Asia* (West Hartford, CT: Kumarian Press, 1990), 172. A similar "amnesty" was issued by the Philippine government in 1975. Whether these amnesties actually encourage migration into forest areas is a matter of debate.
113. Lert Chuntanaparb and Henry I. Wood, *Management of Degraded Forest Land in Thailand* (Bangkok: Kesetsart University, 1986), 41.
114. For a comprehensive overview of existing projects and programs, *see* Lert Chuntanaparb and Henry I. Wood, *Management of Degraded Forest Land in Thailand* (Bangkok: Kesetsart University, 1986); Yongwuth Chalamwong and Gershon Feder, *Land Ownership Security and Land Values in Rural Thailand*, World Bank Staff Working Paper No. 790 (Washington, D.C.: The World Bank, 1986); and Tongroj Onchan, ed., *A Land Policy Study* (Bangkok: Thailand Development Research Foundation, 1990).
115. Author's interview with the RFD Community Forestry Extension and Development Section, November, 1990.

116. Sections 4 and 31 of the 1978 Constitution guarantee Thais equal protection of law. Section 33 requires that "fair compensation shall be paid in due time to the owner" of the property right. "The amount of compensation...shall take into consideration...the mode of acquisition, nature, and condition of the immoveable property, as well as the cause and purpose of the expropriation, so as to serve social justice." Section 18 of the Expropriation of Immoveable Property Act of 1987 requires that "Compensation shall be given to...the legitimate owner or possessor of land to be expropriated."
117. Government of Sri Lanka, 1991, 211, *see* note 81.
118. Ibid, 7.
119. Agrarian Research and Training Institute (ARTI), *Community Forestry Project Baseline Survey* (Colombo, Sri Lanka: ARTI, 1987).
120. Ibid.
121. L. Ostergaard, "Traditional Swidden Cultivators and Forces of Deforestation in Sumatra: The Significance of Local Land Tenure Systems," (presented to the Second Asia-Pacific Consultative Meeting on Biodiversity Conservation, Bangkok, Thailand, February 2–6, 1993).
122. WALHI/LBH (Indonesian Forum for the Environment/Indonesian Legal Aid Institute). *Mistaking Plantations for the Forest: Indonesia's Pulp and Paper Industry, Communities, and Environment* (Jakarta: WALHI/LBH), 1992.
123. Francis J. Seymour, "Social Forestry on Public Lands in Indonesia: A Blurring of Ends and Means," *Social Forestry: Communal and Private Strategies Compared* (Washington, D.C.: The Johns Hopkins University School of Advanced International Studies), 1991, 23–34.
124. *See* e.g., Sopari Wangsadidjaja and Agus Djoko Ismanto, "The Legal Case for Social Forestry in the Production Forests of Indonesia," and Sandra Moniaga, "Toward Community-Based Forestry and Recognition of *Adat* Property Rights in the Outer Islands of Indonesia," in *Legal Frameworks for Forest Management in Asia: Case Studies of Community/State Relations*, Jefferson Fox, ed. (Honolulu: East-West Center), 1993, 115–150.

125. James S. Fingleton, "Conservation, Environment Protection and Customary Land Tenure," *Papua New Guinea Conservation Needs Assessment*, 1993, Vol. 1, 31–56, 43.
126. D. Lamb, *Exploiting the Tropical Rain Forest: An Account of Pulpwood Logging in Papua New Guinea*. Paris: United Nations Educational, Scientific, and Cultural Organization (UNESCO), 1990), 22.
127. World Resources Institute, in collaboration with the United Nations Environment Programme and the United Nations Development Programme, *World Resources 1992–93* (New York: Oxford University Press, 1992), 287 is the source of the smaller estimate, which is based in part on satellite imagery. The larger estimate is found in Table 2.9 (p. 44) of the 1991 *Papua New Guinea National Report*. It includes an estimate of 200,000 hectares a year for the "mainly disturbance" outcomes of subsistence agriculture. *See* p. 42 for additional estimates.
128. World Resources Institute in collaboration with the United Nations Environment Programme and the United Nations Development Programme, *World Resources 1994–95* (New York: Oxford University Press, 1994), 284–285.
129. Philip Shenon, "Isolated Papua New Guineans Fall Prey to Foreign Bulldozers," *The New York Times*, June 5, 1994:A1.
130. The World Conservation Union (IUCN), N. Mark Collins, Jeffrey A. Sayer, and Timothy C. Whitmore, eds., *The Conservation Atlas of Tropical Forests, Asia and the Pacific* (London and Basingstoke: Macmillan Press Ltd., 1991), 178.
131. All production figures taken from: International Tropical Timber Organization (ITTO), *Tropical Forest Management Update*, June 1993, vol. 3, no. 3:12.
132. Commission of Inquiry into Aspects of the Timber Industry in Papua New Guinea, *The Barnett Report* (Hobart, Australia: The Asia-Pacific Action Group, 1990), 18.
133. For a more detailed discussion of these acts, *see* Owen J. Lynch and Allan Marat, "A Review and Analysis of National Laws and Policies Concerning Customary Owners' Rights and the Conservation and Sustainable Development of Forests and Other Biological Resources" in GPNG (Government of Papua New Guinea, Department of Environment and Conservation),

Janis B. Alcorn, ed. *Papua New Guinea Conservation Needs Assessment*, Vol.1 (Landover, MD: Corporate Press, Inc., 1992), 7–30.
134. Chapter No. 205, Sections 5(1) and (2). Emphasis added. The underlined phrases could be read as limiting the extent of customary rights, rather than as a limitation on the State's assertion.
135. A prominent lawyer in Papua New Guinea, Peter Donigi, filed a legal challenge against the national government concerning its assertion of ownership of minerals and petroleum resources. Donigi wanted the court to rule that mineral and petroleum deposits belong to customary resource owners. The case was dismissed in February 1992 in the National Court for lack of standing.
136. Government of Papua New Guinea, *National Forest Policy* (Hohola, Papua New Guinea: Ministry of Forests, 1991).
137. Government of Papua New Guinea, *National Forest Policy* (Hohola, Papua New Guinea: Ministry of Forests, 1991).
138. Government of Papua New Guinea (GOPNG), Department of Environment and Conservation), *Papua New Guinea Conservation Needs Assessment*, Vol. 1. (Landover, MD: Corporate Press, Inc., 1992), 2.
139. *See*, e.g., Owen J. Lynch, "Securing Community-based Tenurial Rights in the Tropical Forests of Asia," *Issues in Development* (Washington, D.C.: World Resources Institute, 1992); Kirk Talbott and Lauren Morris, "Ethnicity and Environment in the Mountains of Laos and Vietnam," *Praxis*, Summer 1993, vol. X, no. 2; Shelton H. Davis, *Indigenous Peoples, Environmental Protection and Sustainable Development* (Gland, Switzerland: International Union for the Conservation of Nature and Natural Resources (IUCN), 1988); Wai Fung Lam, I*nstitutions, Engineering Infrastructure, and Performance in the Governance and Management of Irrigation Systems: The Case of Nepal* (Bloomington: Indiana University Workshop in Political Theory and Analysis, 1994).
140. Theodore Panayotou, *The Economics of Environmental Degradation: Problems, Causes and Responses* (Cambridge, Mass: Harvard Institute for International Development, 1989), 21.

141. Francis J. Seymour and Danilyn Rutherford, "Contractual Agreements for Community-Based Social Forestry Programs in Asia," in Jefferson Fox, ed. *Legal Frameworks for Forest Management in Asia: Case Studies of Community/State Relations*, (Honolulu: East-West Center, 1993), 173–187.
142. Louise Fortmann and Diane Rocheleau, for example, noted that during a workshop on agroforestry, women made "their most valuable contributions and their strongest expressions of interest" during the smaller group activities. "During the frequent and even heated exchanges of questions, answers, criticisms, and suggestions among men in larger sessions, the women were silent—even when topics directly relevant to them...were under discussion." Louise Fortmann and Dianne Rocheleau, "Women and Agroforestry: Four Myths and Three Case Studies," *Agroforestry Systems*, 1990, vol. 2:252–272.
143. S.B. Roy, "Forest Protection Committees in West Bengal, India" in Jefferson Fox, ed., *Legal Frameworks for Forest Management in Asia: Case Studies of Community/State Relations*, Occasional Paper No. 16 (Honolulu: East-West Center, 1993), 19–30.
144. For examples of the working of this dynamic, *see* the case studies in David Western and R. Michael Wright, eds., *Natural Connections: Perspectives in Community-based Conservation* (Washington, D.C. and Covel, CA: Island Press, 1994).
145. Maasai elders resisted entering into a written agreement and this proved to be a "costly mistake given the government's abrogation of every term." David Western, "Ecosystem Conservation and Rural Development: The Case of Amboseli," in David Western and R. Michael Wright, eds., *Natural Connections: Perspectives in Community-based Conservation* (Washington, D.C. and Covelo, CA: Island Press, 1994), 15–52.
146. Despite an agreed-upon revenue sharing formula, the West Bengal community-forest management projects have experienced misunderstandings between local communities and the forest department over how to determine that agreed-upon revenue. Forest Protection Committees agreed to receive 25% of the net sales of timber grown within the joint management area. Difficulties have arisen over how to determine the net.
147. Lynch, 1990, *see* note 10.

BIBLIOGRAPHY

Abdurrahman. *Hukum Adat Menurut Perundang Undangan Republik Indonesia* (Customary Law According to the Legal System of the Republic of Indonesia). Jakarta: Cendana Press, 1984.

Agrarian Research and Training Institute (ARTI). *Community Forestry Project Baseline Survey.* Colomobo, Sri Lanka: ARTI, 1987.

Alcorn, Janice B. and Margery L. Oldfield, eds. *Biodiversity: Culture, Conservation, and Ecodevelopment.* Boulder, CO and London: Westview Press, 1991.

Anderson, Anthony, ed. *Alternatives to Deforestation: Steps Toward Sustainable Use of the Amazon Rain Forest.* New York: Columbia University Press, 1990.

Anon. "Huge Toll from South Asian Floods Tied to Environmental Degradation," *The Christian Science Monitor*, July 29, 1993.

Anon. "Villagers Protest Land Resettlement Programme," *The Bangkok Post*, April 26, 1992.

Anon. "5,000 Die in Floods, Illegal Logging Blamed," *The [Leyte] Reporter*, Nov. 13-19, 1992.

Anon. "Tribes to Get Ancestral Lands," *The Manila Chronicle*, November 24, 1988.

Aplet, Gregory H., Nels Johnson, Jeffrey T. Olson, and V. Alaric Sample, eds. *Defining Sustainable Forestry.* A Wilderness Society Publication. Washington, D.C.: Island Press, 1993.

Arnold, J.E.M. *Community Forestry, Ten Years in Review.* Rome: Food and Agriculture Organization of the United Nations, 1992.

"Arunachal Pradesh's Fading Forests," *Down to Earth*, May 31, 1992, vol. 1, no. 1.

Ascher, William. *Communities and Sustainable Forestry in Developing Countries*. San Francisco: Institute for Contemporary Studies Press, 1995.

The Asia Society. *South Asia and the United States after the Cold War (A Study Mission)*. New York: The Asia Society, 1994.

Asian Development Bank. *Draft Working Paper on Involuntary Resettlement*, 1994.

Bajracharya, Deepak. "Deforestation in the Food/Fuel Context, Historical and Political Perspective from Nepal," *Mountain Research and Development*, Vol. 3, No. 3 (1983), 227–240.

Ball, J. *Indonesian Legal History*. Sydney: Oughtershaw Press, 1982.

Barber, Charles V. *The Legal and Regulatory Framework for Forest Production in Indonesia*. Included as Appendix 1 in Zerner 1990.

Barber, Charles V. and G. Churchill. *Land Policy in Irian Jaya: Issues and Strategies*. Jakarta: Government of Indonesia/United Nations Development Programme, 1987.

Barber, Charles V., Johnson, Nels C., and Emmy Hafild. *Breaking the Logjam: Obstacles to Forestry Policy Reform in Indonesia and the United States*. Washington, D.C.: World Resources Institute, 1994.

Bautista, Germelino M. *Natural Resources, Economics Development and the State, the Philippine Experience*. Singapore: Institute of Southeast Asian Studies, 1994.

Bennett, Gordon. *Aboriginal Rights in International Law*. London: Royal Anthropological Institute, 1978.

Bhattarai, Binod. "Worst Floods in Living Memory Claim Hundreds of Lives," Inter Press Service, July 29, 1993.

Binswanger, Hans P. and Klaus Deininger. *World Bank Land Policy: Evolution and Current Challenges*. Paper prepared for the World Bank Agricultural Sector Symposium. Washington, D.C.: The World Bank, 1994.

Blair, Emma H. and James A. Robertson, eds. *The Philippine Islands, 1493–1898*. 52 Vols. Mandaluyong, Philippines: Cachos Hermanos. 1903–09 (1973 edition).

Borrini, G. *Enhancing People's Participation in the Tropical Forests Action Programme*. Bangkok: Food and Agriculture Organization of the United Nations, 1993.

Brinkman, Willemine, ed. *Why Natural Forests are Linked with Nutrition, Health, and Self-Reliance of Villagers in Northeast Thailand: Phu*

Wiang, Khon Kaen Province. (Fo:DP/THA/84/00w Field Document 6). Bangkok: Royal Forest Department, United Nations Development Programme, and Food and Agriculture Organization of the United Nations, 1989.

Broad, Robin. "The Poor and the Environment: Friends or Foes?" *World Development*, Vol. 22, No. 6 (June 1994), 811–822.

Broad, Robin and John Cavanagh. *Plundering Paradise: The Struggle for the Environment in the Philippines.* Berkeley: University of California Press, 1993.

Bromley, Daniel W. *Environment and Economy: Property Rights and Public Policy.* Oxford: Blackwell, 1991.

——. "Property Relations and Economic Development: The Other Land Reform," *World Development*, Vol. 17, No. 6 (1989), 867–877.

Brown, Lester R. et al. *State of the World 1993: A Worldwatch Institute Report on Progress Toward a Sustainable Society.* New York and London: W. W. Norton and Company, 1993.

Bruce, Johm W. and Shem E. Migot-Adholla, eds. *Searching For Land Tenure Security In Africa.* Dubuque, Iowa: Kendall/Hunt Publishing Company, 1994.

Buhl, Cindy M. *A Citizen's Guide to the Multilateral Development Banks and Indigenous Peoples.* Washington, D.C.: The World Bank, 1994.

Burger, Julian. *Report from the Frontier: The State of the World's Indigenous Peoples.* London and Cambridge, MA: Zed Books Ltd., 1987.

Callister, Debra J. *Illegal Tropical Timber Trade: Asia-Pacific.* Cambridge, U.K.: TRAFFIC International, 1992.

Chamberlain, James L. *Forestry Aspects of Extension. Action Plan for a Private Tree Farm Development Program, Thailand: A Socio-commercial Approach,* Annex 5. Bangkok: PACMAR, Inc. in association with A&R Consultants, 1989.

Chambers, Robert, N.C. Saxena and Tushaan Shah. *To the Hands of the Poor: Water and Trees.* Boulder, CO: Westview Press, 1989.

Chin, S.C. "Do Shifting Cultivators Deforest?" *Forest Resources in the Third World.* Penang, Malaysia: Sahabat Alam Malaysia, 1987.

Chuntanaparb, Lert and Henry I. Wood. *Management of Degraded Forest Land in Thailand.* Bangkok: Kesetsart University, 1986.

Clad, James. *Behind the Myth: Business, Money and Power in Southeast Asia.* London: Grafton Books (a division of Harper Collins Publishers), 1989.

Claiborne, Liz and Art Ortenberg Foundation. *The View from Airlie: Community Based Conservation in Perspective*, Proceedings of the Conference on Community Based Conservation, Airlie, Virginia, (October 17–24, 1993). New York: The Liz Caliborne and Art Ortenberg Foundation, 1994.

Clalammwong, Yongyuth and Gershon Feder. *Land Ownership Security and Land Values in Rural Thailand*, World Bank Staff Working Papers No. 970. Washington, D.C.: The World Bank, 1986.

Clifton, Tony et al. "Choking Cities: Traffic, Pollution, Overcrowding and Disease are Blighting Asia's Boomtowns," *Newsweek* (Japan Edition), May 9, 1994, Vol. CXXIII. No. 19:16.

Coedès, George. *The Indianized States of Southeast Asia*. (Translation of "Histoire Ancienne des États Hindouisés d'Extrême-Orient" (1964)). (An East-West Center Book). Honolulu: The University Press of Hawaii, 1968.

Colchester, Marcus. "Sustaining the Forests: The Community-based Approach in South and South-East Asia," in Draram Ghai, ed., *Development and Change*, Vol. 25, No. 1 (Jan. 1994). The Hague: Blackwell Publishers, 1994.

Colchester, Marcus and Larry Lohmann, eds. *The Struggle for Land and the Fate of the Forests*. Penang, Malaysia: World Rainforest Movement, 1993.

Commission of Inquiry into Aspects of the Timber Industry in Papua New Guinea. *The Barnett Report*. Hobart, Australia: The Asia-Pacific Action Group, 1990.

Conklin, Harold C. *Hanunoo Agriculture: Report on an Integral System of Swidden Cultivation in the Philippines*. Rome: Food and Agriculture Organization of the United Nations, 1957.

——. *Ethnographic Atlas of Ifugao*. New Haven and London: Yale University Press, 1980.

Crawford, James, ed. *The Rights of Peoples*. Oxford: Clarendon Press, 1988.

Cruz, Maria Concepcion, Carrie A. Meyer, Robert Repetto, and Richard Woodward. *Population Growth, Poverty, and Environmental Stress: Frontier Migration in the Philippines and Costa Rica*. Washington, D.C.: World Resources Institute, 1992.

Cruz, Maria Concepcion, Imelda Zosa-Feranil, and Cristela L. Goce. *Population Pressure and Migration: Implications for Upland*

Development in the Philippines. (Working Paper No. 86-06). Los Baños, Philippines: Center for Policy and Development Studies, University of the Philippines at Los Baños, 1986.

Cruz, Wilfrido and Robert Repetto. *The Environmental Effects of Stabilization and Structural Adjustment Programs: The Philippines Case.* Washington, D.C.: World Resources Institute, 1992.

Cushner, Nicholas P. *Landed Estates in the Colonial Philippines.* New Haven, CT: Yale University Southeast Asia Studies. 1976.

Daly, Herman E. and John B. Cobb, Jr. *For the Common Good: Redirecting the Economy Toward Community, the Environment, and a Sustainable Future.* Boston: Beacon Press, 1989.

Davis, Shelton H. *Indigenous Peoples, Environmental Protection and Sustainable Development.* Gland, Switzerland: International Union for the Conservation of Nature and Natural Resources, 1988.

Davis, Shelton H. and Alaka Wali. *Indigenous Territories and Tropical Forest Management in Latin America.* (A Policy, Planning, and Research Working Paper #1100). Washington, D.C.: The World Bank, 1993.

Denniston, Derek. "Defending the Land With Maps," *World Watch*, January/February 1994.

Denslow, Julie and Christine Padoch, eds. *People of the Tropical Rain Forest.* Berkeley: University of California Press, 1988.

Dhagamvar, V. "Rehabilitation: Policy and Institutional Changes Required," in Walter Fernandes and Enakshi Ganguli Thakrul, *Development, Displacement and Rehabilitation* (New Delhi: Indian Social Institute, 1989).

Dove, Michael R. *Foresters' Beliefs About Farmers: A Priority for Social Science Research in Social Forestry.* Honolulu: East-West Center, 1991.

———. "Government Perceptions of Traditional Social Forestry in Indonesia: The History, Causes, and Implications of State Policy on Swidden Agriculture," in *Community Forestry: Socio-Economic Aspects.* Rome: Food and Agriculture Organization of the United Nations, 1985.

———. *Swidden Agriculture in Indonesia: The Subsistence Strategies of the Kalimantan Kantu'.* Berlin: Mouton Press, 1985.

———. Theories of Swidden Agriculture and the Political Economy of Ignorance. *Agroforestry Systems.* The Hague: Martinus Nighoff, 1983, vol. 1:85–99.

Durning, Alan T. "Supporting Indigenous Peoples," in Lester R. Brown et al., *State of the World 1993: A Worldwatch Institute Report on Progress Toward a Sustainable Society.* New York and London: W.W. Norton and Company, 1993.

Eaton, P. *Land Tenure and Conservation: Protected Areas in the South Pacific.* Noumea, New Caledonia: South Pacific Commission, 1985.

Economist Intelligence Unit. *Philippines Country Profile, 1990–1991.* London: The Economist Intelligence Unit, 1991.

Ehrlich, Paul R., Anne H. Ehrlich and Gretchen C. Daily, "Food Security, Population, and Environment," *Population and Development Review*, March 1993, vol. 19, no. 1.

Ekachai, Sanitsuda. *Behind the Smile: Voices of Thailand.* Bangkok: Post Publishing, 1990.

Elwin, Verrier. *A Philosophy for NEFA.* Shillong, 1964.

Erni, Christian. "Mangyan Reject National Park: What Went Wrong with IPAS on Mindoro?" Newsletter: *International Working Group on Indigenous Affairs*, July/August/September, 1993.

Farrington, John and David J. Lewis, eds. *Non-Governmental Organizations and the State in Asia: Rethinking Roles in Sustainable Agricultural Development.* London and New York: Routledge, 1993.

Fingleton, James S. "Conservation, Environment Protection and Customary Land Tenure" in Government of Papua New Guinea, Department of Environment and Conservation, Janis Alcorn ed., *Papua New Guinea Conservation Needs Assessment*, Vol. 1 Landover, MD: Corporate Press, Inc., 1992, 31–56.

Fisher, Roger and William Ury. *Getting to Yes: Negotiating Agreement Without Giving In* (Second Edition). New York: Penquin Books U.S.A. Inc., 1991.

Food and Agriculture Organization of the United Nations. *Forest Resources Assessment 1990: Tropical Countries.* (FAO Forestry Paper No. 112). Rome: FAO, 1993.

——. *Common Forest Resource Management: Annotated Bibliography of Asia, Africa and Latin America.* (Community Forestry Note 11). Rome: FAO, 1993.

Food and Agriculture Organization of the United Nations. Forestry Research Support Program for Asia and the Pacific. *A Coarse and Unedited Search of TREE-CD Abstracts on Community Forestry and Policy/Legislation in E-SE Asia.* Bangkok: FAO Rapa, 1990.

———. *Community Forestry: Rapid Appraisal.* (Community Forestry Note 3). Rome: FAO, 1989.

———. *Forestland for the People: A Forest Village Project in Northeast Thailand.* Rome: FAO, 1987.

———. *Forestry for Local Community Development.* (FAO Forestry Paper No. 7). Rome: FAO, 1978.

Forster, Nancy and David Stanfield. *Tenure Issues and Forest Management: Case Studies in Latin America.* Madison, Wisconsin: University of Wisconsin-Madison, Land Tenure Center, 1993.

Fortmann, Louise and Dianne Rocheleau. "Women and Agroforestry: Four Myths and Three Case Studies," *Agroforestry Systems*, Vol. 2, (1990), 252–272.

Fortmann, Louise and John W. Bruce. *Whose Trees?: Proprietary Dimensions of Forestry.* Boulder, CO: Westview Press, 1988.

Fox, Jefferson. "Forest Resources in a Nepali Village in 1980 and 1990: The Positive Influence of Population Growth," *Mountain Research and Development*, 1993, Vol. 13, No. 1:89–98.

Fox, Jefferson, ed. *Legal Frameworks for Forest Management in Asia: Case Studies of Community/State Relations*, (Occasional Paper No. 16). Honolulu: East-West Center, 1993.

Fox, Jefferson, Owen Lynch, Mark Zimsky, and Erin Moore, eds. *Voices from the Field: Fourth Annual Social Forestry Writing Workshop* (Legal Issues). Honolulu: East-West Center, 1992.

Francisco, Luzviminda Bartolome, and Jonathan Shepard Fast. *Conspiracy for Empire: Big Business, Corruption and the Politics of Imperialism in America, 1876–1907.* Quezon City, Philippines: Foundation for National Studies, 1985.

Gadgil, Madhav. "Draft Background Notes for the Committee on National Forest Policy and Forest (Conservation) Act," (unpublished manuscript (dated 1989) on file at The Centre for Science and Environment in New Delhi).

Gadgil, Madhav and Ramachandra Guha. *This Fissured Land: An Ecological History of India.* New Delhi: Oxford University Press, 1992.

Gilmour, Don and Bob Fisher. *Villagers, Forests, and Foresters: The Philosophy, Process and Practice of Community Forestry in Nepal.* Kathmandu, Nepal: Sahayogi Press, 1991.

González, Nicanor, Francisco Herrera, and Mac Chapin. "Ethnocartography in the Dárien," *Cultural Survival Quarterly*, Winter, 1995.

Goodland, Robert. *Tropical Deforestation: Solutions, Ethics and Religions.* Washington, D.C.: The World Bank, 1991.

Goodland, Robert, Emmanuel O.A. Asibey, Jan C. Post, and Mary B. Dyson. "Tropical Moist Forest Management: The Urgency of Transition to Sustainability," in *Environmental Conservation*, Vol. 17, No. 4. Switzerland: The Foundation for Environmental Conservation, 1990.

Government of Gujurat. *Gujurat Forest Manual, Volume III: Forest Rights, Privileges, Concessions and Cognate Matters.* Ahmedabad: Government of Gujurat Press, 1979.

Government of Indonesia. *Biodiversity Action Plan for Indonesia.* Jakarta: Ministry of National Planning/National Development Planning Agency, 1991.

Government of Papua New Guinea. *Country Report: Papua New Guinea.* Prepared for the South Pacific Heads of Forestry meeting. Port Moresby, Papua New Guinea: Department of Forests, 1990.

Government of Papua New Guinea, Department of Environment and Conservation. *Papua New Guinea Conservation Needs Assessment*, Vol. 1. (Janis B. Alcorn, ed.) Landover, MD: Corporate Press, Inc., 1992.

Government of Sri Lanka. *Natural Resources of Sri Lanka: Conditions and Trends* (A Report Prepared for the Natural Resources, Energy and Science Authority of Sri Lanka). Colombo, Sri Lanka: Keells Business Systems, Ltd., 1991.

——. *Report of the Land Commission, 1987.* Colombo, Sri Lanka: Department of Government Printing, 1990.

Government of Thailand, National Economic and Social Development Board/United States Agency for International Development. *Safeguarding the Future: Restoration and Sustainable Development in the South of Thailand.* Bangkok: Government of Thailand, USAID, 1989.

Grandstaff, Terry. *Shifting Cultivation in Northern Thailand.* Tokyo: United Nations Press, 1980.

Haeruman, H. "Masalah Sosial dalam Pembangunan Kehutanan" (Social Problems in Forestry Development). *Andal*, No. 12 (1992). Jakarta. (translated by Chip Barber).

Hall, D.G.E. *A History of South-East Asia.* New York: St. Martin's Press, 1981.

Hardin, Garrett. "The Tragedy of the Commons". *Science*, 1968, 162: 1243–48.

Hendrix, Steven E. *Property Law Innovation in Latin America with Recommendations*. Madison, WI: Land Tenure Center, May 1993.

Hirsch, Philip. "Forests, Forest Preserves, and Forest Land in Thailand," *The Geographical Journal*, 1989, vol. 156, no. 2:166–74.

Hoamuangkaew, Wuthipol, Prin Sri-Anan and Lert Chuntanaparb. *Agro-Forestry in Tab Lan Forest Communities, Soeng Sang, Nakhon Ratchasima, Northeast Thailand*. (KU/Ford Foundation 870-0535, Working Document No. 7). Bangkok: Kesetsart University's Northeast Thailand Upland Social Forestry Project, 1988.

Hohfeld, Wesley N. "Fundamental Legal Conceptions as Applied in Judicial Reasoning," *Yale Law Journal*, 1917, vol. 26:710.

Hong, Evelyn. "Forest Destruction and the Plight of Sarawak's Natives," *Forest Resources*.

Indonesian Forum for the Environment/Indonesian Legal Aid Institute (WALHI/LBH). *Mistaking Plantations for the Forest: Indonesia's Pulp and Paper Industry, Communities, and Environment*. Jakarta: WALHI/LBH, 1992.

Indonesian Legal Aid Foundation (YLBHI). *The Torching of the Peoples' Homes and the Destruction of Their Fields in Subdistrict Pulau Panggung, Lampung Selatan, Sumatra, Indonesia*. Jakarta: YLBHI, 1989.

International Development Center of Japan. *Local Dimensions of Environmental Management: Analyses of Malaysian Institutions and Cases*, A Report Prepared for the Ministry of Foreign Affairs. Tokyo: International Development Center of Japan, 1993.

International Tropical Timber Organization. *Tropical Forest Management Update*, Vol. 3, No. 3 (June 1993) 10–12.

International Work Group for Indigenous Affairs/Centre for Development Research (IWGIA/CDR). *"...Never Drink From the Same Cup": Proceedings of the Conference on Indigenous Peoples in Africa, Tune, Denmark, June 1–3, 1993*. CDR-IWGIA Document No. 74. Copenhagen: IWGIA/CDR, 1993.

Jodha, N. S. *Common Property Resources: A Missing Dimension of Development Strategies*. World Bank Discussion Papers #169. Washington, D.C.: The World Bank, 1992.

Johnson, Nels and Bruce Cabarle. *Surviving the Cut: Natural Forest Management in the Humid Tropics.* Washington, D.C.: World Resources Institute, 1993.

Joshi, A.L. "Nationalization of Forest in Nepal: Why was it Needed?," *The Nepal Journal of Forestry,* October 1991, vol. VII, no. 1.

Justimbaste, Emil. "5,000 Die in Floods, Illegal Logging Blamed." *The Reporter* (Manila), Nov. 13–19, 1991.

Kalipunan ng mga Katutubong Mamamayan ng Pilipinas (KAMP). *Ancestral Domain Rights and the IFP; A Briefing paper of the Plight of the Ata-Manobo in Talaingod, Davao Del Norte against a Major Aggressor, Alcantara and Sons, Inc. (ALSONS).* Quezon City: Kalipunan ng mga Katutubong Mamamayan ng Pilipinas, 1995.

Khadka, Shantam S. and Surya K. Gurung. *Popular Management of Forest Resources in Selected Districts of Rapti Zone: Review of Laws and Regulations on Forestry User Groups.* Kathmandu, Nepal: Center for Economic Development and Administration, Tribhuvan University, 1990.

Kummer, David M. *Deforestation in the Postwar Philippines.* Quezon City, Philippines: Ateneo de Manila University Press, 1992.

Kummer, David M. "The Political Use of Philippine Forestry Statistics in the Postwar Period," *Crime, Law & Social Change* (1995), vol. 22, no. 163:180.

Kunstadter, Peter, E.C. Chapman, and Sanga Sabhasri. *Farmers in the Forest: Economic Development and Marginal Agriculture in Northern Thailand.* Honolulu: University of Hawaii, 1978.

Lamb, D. *Exploiting the Tropical Rain Forest: An Account of Pulpwood Logging in Papua New Guinea.* Paris: United Nations Educational, Scientific, and Cultural Organization (UNESCO), 1990.

Lanley, Jean-Paul. *Tropical Forest Resources.* (FAO Forestry Paper No. 30). Rome: Food and Agriculture Organization of the United Nations, 1982.

Legal Rights and Natural Resources Center-Kasama sa Kalikasan/ Friends of the Earth-Philippines (LRC-KSK). *Ancestral Domain Rights and the IFP.* Quezon City, Philippines: LRC-KSK, 1995.

——. *From Timber License Agreements to Sustainable Forestry Agreements: Continuing Unsustainability and Inequity in Philippine Forest Policy, A Special Report.* Quezon City, Philippines: LRC-KSK, 1995.

Leungaramsri, Pinkaew and Noel Rajesh, eds. *The Future of People and Forests in Thailand After the Logging Ban.* Bangkok: Project for Ecological Recovery, 1992.

Lindley, Mark F. *The Acquisition and Government of Backward Territory in International Law Being a Treatise on the Law and Practice Relating to Colonial Expansion.* London: Longmans, Green, 1926.

Little, Peter D. and Michael M. Horowitz, eds. *Lands at Risk in the Third World: Local-level Perspectives.* Boulder, CO and London: Westview Press, 1987.

Lynch, Owen J. *Colonial Legacies in a Fragile Republic: A History of Philippine Land Law and State Formation with Emphasis on the Early U.S. Regime (1898–1913),* J.S.D. (Doctor of Laws) dissertation, Yale University Law School, 1992.

———. "Securing Community-based Tenurial Rights in the Tropical Forests of Asia," *Issues in Development Report.* Washington, D.C.: World Resources Institute, 1992.

———. "Whither the People? Demographic, Tenurial, and Agricultural Aspects of the Tropical Forestry Action Plan," *Issues in Development Report.* Washington, D.C.: World Resources Institute, 1990.

———. "Indigenous Rights in Insular Southeast Asia," in Ruth Taswell, ed., *Southeast Asian Tribal Groups and Ethnic Minorities: Prospects for the Eighties and Beyond.* Cambridge, MA: Cultural Survival, Inc., 1987, 27–46.

Lynch, Owen J. and Janis B. Alcorn. "Tenurial Rights and Community-based Conservation," in David Western and R. Michael Wright, eds., *Natural Connections: Perspectives in Community-based Conservation.* Washington, D.C. and Covelo, CA: Island Press, 1994, 373–392.

Lynch, Owen J. and Allan Marat. "A Review and Analysis of National Laws and Policies Concerning Customary Owners' Rights and the Conservation and Sustainable Development of Forests and Other Biological Resources" in Government of Papua New Guinea, Department of Environment and Conservation, Janis B. Alcorn, ed., *Papua New Guinea Conservation Needs Assessment, Vol. 1* Landover, MD: Corporate Press, Inc., 1992, 7–30.

Lynch, Owen J. and Kirk Talbott. "Legal Responses to the Philippine Deforestation Crises," *Journal of International Law and Politics,* vol. 20, no. 3, 1988.

Martin, Fentin. "Common Pool Resources and Collective Action: A Bibliography," prepared for the Workshop in Political Theory and Policy Analysis, January 1989. Bloomington, Ind.: Indiana University.

Marten, Gerald. *Traditional Agriculture in Southeast Asia: A Human Ecology Perspective*. 1986.

McDougal, M. and W. M. Reisman, eds., International Court of Justice. "Western Sahara," *The Hague: International Law in Contemporary Perspective*. Mineola, NY: Foundation Press, 1975.

McDougal, Myers and W. Michael Reisman, eds., *International Law in Contemporary Perspective*. Mineola, NY: Foundation Press, 1981.

Media Mindanao News Service Investigative Team. *Ethnocide: Is it Real?* Davao City, Philippines: Media Mindanao News Service, Inc., 1993.

Miller, Kenton and Laura Tangley. *Trees of Life: Saving Tropical Forests and Their Biological Wealth*. Boston: Beacon Press, 1991.

Miller, Marc S. et al. *State of the Peoples: A Global Human Rights Report on Societies in Danger*. Boston: Beacon Press, 1993.

Ministry of Agriculture and Cooperatives Royal Forest Department. *Thai Forestry Master Plan*, vol. 5:85. Bangkok: Ministry of Agriculture and Cooperatives Royal Forest Department, 1993.

Moniaga, Sandra. "Towards Community-Based Forestry and Recognition of Adat Property Rights in the Outer Islands of Indonesia: A Legal and Policy Analysis," in Jefferson Fox, ed. *Legal Frameworks for Forest Management in Asia: Case Studies of Community/State Relations*, Honolulu: East-West Center, 1993.

Murphee, Marshall W. "The Role of Institutions," in David Western and R. Michael Wright, eds. *Natural Connections: Perspectives in Community-based Conservation*. Washington, D.C. and Covelo, CA: Island Press, 1994. 403–427.

Olafson, Harold, ed. *Adaptive Strategies and Change in Philippine Swidden-based Societies*. Los Baños, Philippines: Forestry Research Institute, 1981.

Oldfield, Margery L. and Janis B. Alcorn, eds. *Biodiversity: Culture, Conservation, and Ecodevelopment*. Boulder, CO: Westview Press, 1991.

Onchan, Tongroj, ed. *A Land Policy Study*. Bangkok: Thailand Development Research Foundation, 1990.

Ostergaard, L. "Traditional Swidden Cultivators and Forces of Deforestation in Sumatra: The Significance of Local Land Tenure Systems," presented to the Second Asia-Pacific Consultative Meeting on Biodiversity Conservation, Bangkok, Thailand, February 2–6, 1993.

Ostrom, Elinor. *Governing the Commons: The Evolution of Institutions for Collective Action*. Cambridge, U.K: Cambridge University Press, 1990.

Ostrom, Elinor, Roy Gardner, and James Walker. *Rules, Games, & Common-Pool Resources*. Ann Arbor: University of Michigan Press, 1994.

Panayotou, Theodore. *The Economics of Environmental Degradation: Problems, Causes and Responses*. Cambridge, Mass: Harvard Institute for International Development, 1989.

Pathy, Haganath. "Shifting Cultivators of India: Bearing the Brunt of Development," *Forest Resources in the Third World*.

Peluso, Nancy Lee. *Rich Forests, Poor People and Development: Forest Access Control and Resistance in Java*. Berkeley: University of California Press, 1990.

Peluso, Nancy Lee, Matt Turner, and Louise Fortmann. *Introducing Community Forestry: Annotated Listing of Topics and Readings* (Community Forestry Note No. 12). Rome: Food and Agriculture Organization of the United Nations, 1994.

Pelzer, Karl J. *Pioneer Settlement in the Asiatic Tropics: Studies in Land Utilization and Agricultural Colonization in Southeast Asia*. New York: American Geographical Society. 1945.

Perlin, John. *A Forest Journey: The Role of Wood in the Development of Civilization*. New York and London: W.W. Norton & Company, 1989.

Peraturan Pemerintah No. 21/1970 tentang Hak Pengusahaan Hutan dan Hak Pemungutan Hasil Hutan [Government Regulation No. 21/1970 concerning the Right of Forest Exploitation and the Right to Harvest Forest Products].

Phelan, John L. *The Hispanicization of the Philippines: Spanish Aims and Filipino Responses*. Madison, WI: University of Wisconsin Press. 1959.

Philippine Department of Environment and Natural Resources (DENR). *Philippine Forestry Statistics*. Quezon City: Forest Management Bureau, 1993.

Pimbert, Michel P. and Jules N. Pretty. *Parks, People and Professionals: Putting "Participation" into Protected Area Management* (United Nations Research Institute for Social Development Discussion Paper No. 57). Geneva: United Nations Research Institute for Social Development, 1995.

Plehn, Carl C. "Taxation in the Philippines," *Political Science Quarterly*, 1901–02 16:680–711 and 17:125–48.

Poffenberger, Mark. "The Resurgence of Community Forestry Management in Eastern India," in David Western and R. Michael Wright, eds. *Natural Connections: Perspectives in Community-based Conservation.* Washington, D.C. and Covelo, CA: Island Press, 1994, 53–79.

———. "The Resurgence of Community Forest Management in the Jungle Mahals of West Bengal," presented to the Conference on South Asia's Changing Environment, Bolagio, Italy, March 16-20, 1992.

Poffenberger, Mark, ed. *Keepers of the Forest: Land Management Alternatives in Southeast Asia.* West Hartford, CT: Kumarian Press, 1989.

Poffenberger, Mark and Betsy McGean. *Policy Dialogue on Natural Forest Regeneration and Community Management*, proceedings of a workshop held 2–4 March, 1994 in Honolulu, HI. The Asia Sustainable Forest Management Network, Research Network Report, Number 5 (April 1994). Honolulu: The East-West Center, 1994.

Pongsapich, Amara. *Action Plan for a Private Tree Farm Development Program, Thailand: A Socio-Commercial Approach.* Socio-Economic Aspects, Annex 10. Bangkok: PACMAR, Inc., (in association with A&R Consultants), 1989.

Poole, Peter. *Developing a Partnership of Indigenous Peoples, Conservationists and Land Use Planners in Latin America.* (A World Bank Policy, Planning, and Research Working Paper). Washington, D.C.: The World Bank, 1989.

———. "Indigenous Peoples, Mapping, and Biodiversity Conservation: A Survey of Current Activities." Washington, D.C.: The Biodiversity Support Program (forthcoming, 1995).

Poore, Duncan et al. *No Timber Without Trees: Sustainability in the Tropical Forest.* London: Earthscan Publications Ltd., 1989.

Postel, Sandra. "Carrying Capacity: Earth's Bottom Line," in Lester R. Brown, ed., *State of the World 1994: A Worldwatch Institute Re-*

port on Progress Toward a Sustainable Society. New York and London: W. W. Norton & Co., 1994. 3–21.

Pragtong, Kamon and David E. Thomas. "Evolving Management Systems in Thailand," in Mark Poffenberger, ed., *Keepers of the Forest: Land Management Alternatives in Southeast Asia.* West Hartford, CT: Kumarian Press, 1990. 167–186.

Prajapati, T.B. "Private Forestry in Nepal," presented to the Second National Community Forestry Workshop in Kathmandu, February, 22–25, 1993, and printed in *Banko Janakari* (A Journal of Forestry Information for Nepal) March 1993, vol. 4, no. 1, Kathmandu, Nepal: The Department of Forestry and Plant Research, His Majesty's Government of Nepal, 1993.

Pramano, A.H. *A Brief Overview on Forest Land Use and Deforestation in Indonesia.* Jakarta: Wahana Lingkungan Hidup Indonesia, 1991.

Rambo, Terry. "Slash and Burn Farmers: Villains or Victims?," *Earthwatch*, 1993, no. 39.

Regmi, Mahesh C. *Land Tenure and Taxation in Nepal.* Bibliotheca Himalayica Series 1, vol. 26. Kathmandu: Ratna Pustak Bhandar, 1978.

——. Landownership in Nepal. Berkeley and Los Angeles: University of California Press, 1976.

Reid, Walter V. and Kenton R. Miller. *Keeping Options Alive: The Scientific Basis for Conserving Biodiversity.* Washington, D.C., World Resources Institute, 1989.

Reisman, W. Michael. "Protecting Indigenous Rights in International Adjudication," *American Journal of International Law*, Vol. 89, pp. 341–62 (1995).

Rensberger, Boyce. "Out of Africa 1.8 Million Years Ago? 'Java Man' Fossils Older Than Thought" in *The Washington Post*, February 24, 1994, p. A4.

Repetto, Robert. *The "Second India" Revisited: Population, Poverty, and Environmental Stress Over Two Decades.* Washington, D.C.: World Resources Institute, 1994.

Repetto, Robert. *The Forest for the Trees? Government Policies and the Misuse of Forest Resources.* Washington, D.C.: World Resources Institute, 1988.

Repetto, Robert, ed. *The Global Possible: Resources, Development, and the New Century.* A World Resources Institute Book. New Haven and London: Yale University Press, 1985.

Repetto, Robert and Malcolm Gillis. *Public Policies and the Misuse of Forest Resources*. New York: Cambridge University Press, 1989.

RePPProT [Regional Physical Planning Programme for Transmigration]. *The Land Resources of Indonesia: A National Overview*. Jakarta: Overseas Development Administration (UK) and Department of Transmigration (Indonesia), 1990.

Rojanalak, Disathat. "Concrete Jungle on Forest Reserve Dilemma for Authorities," *The Bangkok Post*, November 11, 1990.

———. "Time for Villagers to Have Their Say in Forming Policy," *The Bangkok Post*, November 11, 1990.

Roy, S.B. "Forest Protection Committees in West Bengal, India" in Jefferson Fox, ed., *Legal Frameworks for Forest Management in Asia: Case Studies of Community/State Relations*, Occasional Paper No. 16. Honolulu: East-West Center, 1993.

Roychowdhury, Anumita. "Chopping Down the Future," *Down to Earth*, May 31, 1992.

Rush, James. *The Last Tree: Reclaiming the Environment in Tropical Asia*. New York: The Asia Society, 1991.

Sanguantam, P., Lert Chuntanaparb, and P. Prasomsin. *Multi-Resource Inventories in Dong Mun Forest Communities, Northeast Thailand*. Working Document No. 3.). Bangkok, Thailand: Kesetsart University/Ford Foundation, 1988.

Santasombat, Yos. "Community Forestry Legislation in Thailand," presented to the Workshop on Legal Issues in Social Forestry sponsored by The Ford Foundation, Bali, Indonesia, November 4–6, 1991.

Sarin, Madhu. "Regenerating India's Forests: Reconciling Gender Equity with Joint Forest Management," presented to the International Workshop on India's Forest Management and Ecological Revival, New Delhi, India, February 10–12, 1994.

———. *From Conflicts to Collaboration: Local Institutions in Joint Forest Management*, Joint Forest Management Working Paper No. 14 (New Delhi: National Support Group for Joint Forest Management, Society for Promotion of Wastelands Development and The Ford Foundation, 1993.

Serrano, Isagani R. *Civil Society in the Asia-Pacific Region*. Washington, D.C.: Civicus, 1994.

Seymour, Francis J. "Are Successful Community Based Conservation Projects Designed or Discovered?" in David Western and R. Michael Wright, eds., *Natural Connections: Perspectives in Community-Based Conservation*. Washington, D.C. and Covelo, CA: Island Press, 1994, 472–496.

———. "Social Forestry on Public Lands in Indonesia: A Blurring of Means and Ends?" in *Social Forestry: Communal and Private Management Strategies Compared*, Case Studies Presented at a Conference, February 14, 1991. (Washington, D.C.: Program on Social Change and Development, The Paul H. Nitze School of Advanced International Studies of The Johns Hopkins University, 1991), 23–34.

Seymour, Francis J. and Danilyn Rutherford, "Contractual Agreements for Community-Based Social Forestry Programs in Asia," in Jefferson Fox, ed. *Legal Frameworks for Forest Management in Asia: Case Studies of Community/State Relations*. Honolulu: East-West Center, 1993, 173–187.

Sharma, B.D. *29th Report of the Commissioner for Scheduled Castes and Scheduled Tribes*. Faridabad: Government of India Press, 1989.

Sharma, Narenda P., ed. *Managing the World's Forests: Looking for Balance between Conservation and Development*. Dubuque, IA: Kendall/Hunt Publishing Company, 1992.

Sheehan, Nancy. *Gender and Natural Resource Tenure Research*, workshop proceedings. Madison, WI: Land Tenure Center, University of Wisconsin-Madison, June 1992.

Shenon, Philip. "Isolated Papua New Guineans Fall Prey to Foreign Bulldozers," *The New York Times*, June 5, 1994, p. A1.

Social Research Institute of Chiang Mai University, Research and Development Institute of Khon Kaen University, Non-Governmental Organization Co-ordinating Committee on Rural Development (NGO-CORD), Northern and Northeastern Chapters, and Local Development Institute. *Community Forestry: Declaration of the Customary Rights of Local Communities: Thai Democracy at the Grassroots*, Results of the "Community Forestry in Thailand:Development Perspectives" workshop, held at the Women Studies Center of the Social Sciences Faculty, Chiang Mai University, June 27–28, 1992.

Society for Legal and Environmental Analysis and Development Research (LEADERS), Faculty of Law, Tribhuvan University, and Women in Environment. *Proceedings of the International Conference on Environment and Law, 6–8 March, 1992, Kathmandu, Nepal.* Kathmandu, Nepal: LEADERS, 1992.

Solheim, William G. II, "New Light on a Forgotten Past," *National Geographic,* March 1971, vol. 139, no. 3, 330–339.

Spencer, J.E. *Shifting Cultivation in Southeast Asia.* Berkeley: University of California Press, 1966.

Sturtevant, David R. *Popular Uprisings in the Philippines, 1840–1940.* Ithaca, NY: Cornell University Press, 1976.

Sudiyat, I. *Hukum Adat* (Customary Law). Yogyakarta, Indonesia: Liberty, 1981.

Talbott, Kirk. "Implementing the Convention on Biological Diversity: Developing Linkages with Local Communities,"*Thailand Development Research Institute Quarterly Review,* June 1995, vol. 10. No. 2, 13–19.

——. "Central Africa's Forests: The Second Greatest Forest System on Earth," *Issues in Development.* Washington, D.C.: World Resources Institute, 1993.

——. "Nation States and Forest Peoples: Tenurial Control and the Squandering of the Central African Rainforest," (Draft). Prepared for presentation at the Second Annual Meeting of the International Assoc. for the Study of Common Property in Winnipeg, Canada, Sept. 26–29, 1991.

Talbott, Kirk and Shantam Khadka. "Handing it Over: An Analysis of the Legal and Policy Framework of Community Forestry in Nepal," *Cases in Development.* Washington, D.C.: World Resources Institute, 1994.

Talbott, Kirk and Lauren Morris. "Ethnicity and Environment in the Mountains of Laos and Vietnam," *Praxis: The Fletcher School Journal of Development Studies,* Summer 1993, vol. X, no. 2, 85–95.

Taylor-Powell, Ellen (in collaboration with Andrew Manu, Stephen C. Geiger, Mamadou Ouattara, and Anthony S. R. Juo). "Integrated Management of Agricultural Watersheds: Land Tenure and Indigenous Knowledge of Soil and Crop Management," *TropSoils Bulletin 91-04,* November 1991. Bryan, TX: Soil Management Collaborative Research Support Program.

Thailand Development Research Institute (TDRI). *Thailand Natural Resources Profile: Is the Resource Base for Thailand's Development*

Sustainable? Bangkok: Thailand Development Research Institute, 1987.

Thiesenhusen, William, C. "Implications of the Rural Land Tenure System for the Environmental Debate: Three Scenarios," *The Journal of Developing Areas*, October 1991, vol. 26, no. 1:1–23.

Thorburn, Craig. "The Cultural and Political Context of Mapping Indigenous Forest Tenure Systems in Indonesia," report submitted to The Biodiversity Support Program, 1994.

Thrupp, Lori Ann. "Legitimizing Local Knowledge; From Displacement to Empowerment for Third World People," *Agriculture and Human Values*, Gainesville, FL: University of Florida, 1989.

Thrupp, Lori Ann with Arleen Mayorga. "Engendering Central American Forestry Management: The Integration of Women In Forest Policy Initiatives," *Issues in Development*. Washington, D.C.: World Resources Institute, 1994.

Tukahirwa, Eldad and Peter G. Veit. "Public Policy and Legislation in Environmental Management: Terracing in Nyarurembo, Uganda," *From the Ground Up Case Study Series - No. 5*. Nairobi: World Resources Institute and ACTS Press, 1992.

Umans, L.H.M. *Analysis and Typology of Indigenous Forest Management in the Humid Tropics of Asia*. (Werkdocument IKC- NBLF Nr. 26). Wageningen, The Netherlands: National Reference Centre for Nature, Forests and Landscape, 1993.

United Nations Educational Scientific and Cultural Organization (UNESCO). *Swidden Cultivation in Asia, Volume Three*. Bangkok, Thailand: UNESCO Regional Office for Education in Asia and the Pacific, 1985.

United Nations Environment Programme (UNEP). *Environmental Data Report 1993–94*. Oxford, U.K.: Blackwell Publishers, 1993.

U.S. Supreme Court. Cariño v. Insular Government. United States Reports (1909) 212:449.

Usher, Ann Danaiya. "Huay Kaew: Broken Promises," *The Nation*, September 20, 1991.

Utting, Peter. *Trees, People and Power*. London: Earthscan, 1993.

Varanien, Ploenpoch. "Land Resettlement Compromise Reached," 1992.

Visetbhakdi, Norani. "Deforestation and Reforestation in Thailand," *Bangkok Bank Monthly Review*, June 1989. 241–51.

Vitoria, Francisco de. *Address in Commemoration of His Lectures.* Washington, D.C.: Catholic University of America, 1539.

Vitug, Marites Danguilan. *The Politics of Logging: Power from the Forest.* Manila: Philippine Center for Investigative Journalism, 1993.

Von Furer-Haimendorf, Christoph. *Tribes of India: The Struggle for Survival.* Oxford: Oxford University Press, 1982.

Wai, Fung Lam. *Institutions, Engineering Infrastructure, and Performance in the Governance and Management of Irrigation Systems: The Case of Nepal* (doctoral dissertation). Bloomington, IN: Workshop in Political Theory and Policy Analyis, Indiana University, 1994.

Wangsadidjaja, Sopari and Agus Djoko Ismanto, "The Legal Case for Social Forestry in the Production Forests of Indonesia," in Jefferson Fox, ed. *Legal Frameworks for Forest Management in Asia: Case Studies of Community/State Relations*, Honolulu: East-West Center, 1993.

Warner, Katherine. *Shifting Culivators: Local Technical Knowledge and Natural Resource Management in the Humid Tropics.* Rome: Food and Agriculture Organization of the United Nations, 1991.

Weinstock, Joseph. "Land Tenure Practices of the Swidden Cultivators of Borneo," Master's Thesis, Cornell University, 1979.

Weiss, Edith Brown. *In Fairness to Future Generations: International Law, Common Patrimony, and Intergenerational Equity.* Tokyo: The United Nations University, 1989.

Wells, Michael and Katrina Brandon. *Parks and People.* Washington, D.C.: The World Bank, 1992.

Western, David. "Ecosystem Conservation and Rural Development: The Case of Amboseli," in David Western and R. Michael Wright, eds., (Shirley C. Strum, Associate Editor). *Natural Connections: Perspectives in Community-based Conservation.* Washington, D.C. and Covelo, CA: Island Press, 1994. 15–52.

Westoby, Jack. *Introduction to World Forestry.* Oxford: Basil Blackwell, 1988.

Winzeler, R.L. "Ecology, Culture, Social Organization, and State Formation in Southeast Asia," *Current Anthropology*, 1974 17:4ff.

World Bank. *Resettlement and Development: The Bankwide Review of Projects Involving Involuntary Resettlement 1986–1993.* Washington, D.C.: The World Bank, 1994.

———. *Philippines: Environment and Natural Resource Management Study*. Washington, D.C.: The World Bank. 1989.

World Bank Staff Working Papers No. 70. Washington, D.C.: The World Bank, 1986.

The World Conservation Union (IUCN) (Mark N. Collins, Jeffrey A. Sayer, and Timothy C. Whitmore, eds.). *The Conservation Atlas of Tropical Forests, Asia and the Pacific*. London and Basingstoke: Macmillan Press Ltd., 1991.

World Resources Institute, the World Conservation Union (IUCN), and United Nations Environment Programme. *Global Biodiversity Strategy: Guidelines for Action to Save, Study, and Use Earth's Biotic Wealth Sustainably and Equitably*. Washington, D.C.: World Resources Institute, 1992.

World Resources Institute in collaboration with the United Nations Environment Programme and the United Nations Development Programme. *World Resources 1994–5: A Guide to the Global Environment*. New York: Oxford University Press, 1994.

World Wildlife Fund for Nature/Indonesia. "Participatory Tools for Community-Forest Profiling and Zonation of Conservation Areas, Experiences from the Kayan Mentarang Nature Reserve, East Kalimantan, Indonesia," July 1994.

Yano, Toru. "Land Tenure in Thailand," *Asian Survey*. 1968, 8(10), 853–863.

Zerner, Charles. "Through a Green Lens: Construction of Customary Environmental Law and Community in Indonesia's Maluku Island." *Law and Society Review*. Volume 28, No. 5. 1994.

———. *Indigenous Forest-Dwelling Communities in Indonesia's Outer Islands: Livelihoods, Rights, and Environmental Management Institutions in the Era of Industrial Forest Exploitation*. 1992.

———. "Community Rights, Customary Law, and the Law of Timber Concession in Indonesia's Forest: Legal Option and Alternative in Designing the Commons." *Jakarta Forestry Studies* UTF/IN/065. 1990.

———. *Legal Options for the Indonesian Forestry Sector*. Jakarta: Government of Indonesia/United Nations Food and Agriculture Organization, 1990.

ORDER FORM

ORDER ADDITIONAL COPIES NOW
and receive a 10% discount

__ YES, please send me ____ copies of **Balancing Acts: Community-Based Forest Management and National Law in Asia and the Pacific** at the special discount price of $22.45, plus $3.50 shipping and handling.

Payment Information:
__ Check enclosed in the amount of: $_____
__ Please charge my credit card:
___ Visa ___ MasterCard
Account Number: _____
Expiration Date: _____
Signature _____

Ship to:
Name: _____
Address: _____
City, State, Zip Code: _____
Daytime Phone: _____

In a hurry? Order by phone with a Visa or MasterCard by calling 1-800-822-0504, or 410-516-6963.

__ Please check here if you would like to receive a complete catalog of WRI publications.

Return this form with payment, to: WRI Publications, P.O. Box 4852, Hampden Station, Baltimore, MD 21211. All orders must be prepaid. Prices subject to change without notice.